Quantum Creativity

DATE DUE

OC 04

MR 22 '05

JE 23 08

DEMCO 38-296

"*Quantum* ... clarify-
ing how t ... ndable
and full o ... is book
is a must ... ssibilities
in their w ... t a few
highlighte

Thinking
Mental

"A growin ... success
needs emp ... the busi-
ness, and ... passion
for life. *Qu* ... their
own uniqu

"I speak to ... t
change. No ... nge and
being thei ... power-
ful tools to ... d find
bright opp

adio and
speaker

"*Quantum Creativity* is an exhilerating ride through the country-
side of creative possibilities. It's a great tool to stimulate creative
capabilities at all levels of an organization."

— LARRY MYATT, Vice President, SPS Payment Systems, Inc.

Quantum Creativity

Pamela Meyer

CHICAGO, ILLINOIS

...print from the following:

...right © 1994, Anne Lamott.

...*mpany Magazine,* Special
Collector's Edition, Vol. 1. Reprinted by permission of the publisher.

"Thoughts on Theatre: An Interview with John Glover and Cherry Jones,"
Equity News, September 1995. Copyright © 1995. Reprinted by permission of
the publisher.

The Universe is a Green Dragon, Brian Swimme. Bear & Co. Copyright © 1984,
Bear & Co.

Truth in Comedy, Charna Halpern, Del Close, and Kim "Howard" Johnson.
Meriweather Publishing. Copyright © 1993, Meriweather Publishing.

Cover, text design and layout by Maria Baseleon, Studio M Design, Inc., Chicago

Library of Congress Card Catalog Number: 97-91009.

ISBN 0-9660114-0-6

First Printing, 1997

Printed in the United States of America

Quantum Creativity™ is a trademark of Meyer Creativity Associates, Inc.

Acknowledgements

This book could not have happened without the support and collective wisdom of the many people who have walked with me (and ahead of me) on this mystery tour of life.

For their invaluable cheerleading and response to early drafts I thank Amy Opalk, Michele Estrada Feigin, Joyce Cole, Ann Folwell Stanford, Ph.D., Patricia Monaghan, Ph.D., Mary Cross, Sara Wolfersberger, Janis Cole, Michael Hammermiester, Sarah Bradley, Barbara Langer, Ph.D., Kate Goehring, Ellen Credille, David Jensen, and Izzy Gesell.

I thank my fierce friends and champions Cheri Coons, Allison Morgan, Susan McGury, and Nancy Nickel for being with me on this and so many other creative life adventures. Giganitic love to my mother, Rachel Meyer, who has inspired and supported my creativity from the very start.

Because I hope to always remember that I am first a student, I must thank only a few of the teachers who have encouraged me and shared their wisdom with me at important turning points in my life: Judith Schneebeck, His Holiness Maharishi Mahesh Yogi, and Anne Wilson Schaef, Ph.D.

I also shower gratitude on the many past workshop participants and former students who shared so much of their own experience and inspiration with me (some of which they kindly allowed me to reprint in this book) and whom were truly instrumental in the development of these principles.

Table of Contents

"We are at that very point in time when a 400-year-old age is dying and another is struggling to be born—a shift of culture, science, society, and institutions enormously greater than the world has ever experienced. Ahead, the possibility of the regeneration of individuality, liberty, community, and ethics such as the world has never known, and a harmony with nature, with one another, and with the divine intelligence such as the world has never dreamed."

—DEE WARD HOCK, Founder of Visa

Introduction

We don't need to be taught how to be creative. We already know how; each of us has all of the resources to live a rich life, full of wonder and possibility. While we *can* learn problem-solving and idea-generating techniques effective in response to a particular problem or issue, these models should not be mistaken for creativity itself. They help focus and channel what is already there. This book is about rediscovering what is already there.

Expanding life's creative possibilities is more than "freeing the artist within." Unfortunately our mechanistic worldview entices us to compartmentalize ourselves. If we were good at painting, acting, music or any of the other fine arts, we were labeled "creative" at an early age. If we didn't express our creativity in one of these ways, we got some other label—"organized," "outgoing," "good with numbers." For some of us, creativity was the luxury of others.

Many of us continue to live comfortably in these boxes for our entire lives. Others eventually find the box painfully confining and must break out of it for survival. How do we breakout? Embrace new principles. Deepak Chopra says,

"Our world view creates our world."[1] Our worldview (or paradigm) is made up of our past experiences and beliefs. It is the system through which we filter each new experience. Many of us have learned false beliefs which have, in turn, given us a false worldview—one that is stifling to our creative life.

Business has embraced hard-hitting words like innovation, thinking out of the box, and Edward DeBono's "lateral thinking" as respectable alternatives to dangerously soft sounding "creativity." Understandably, businesses tend to focus on the practical outcomes of creativity—new product development and improved bottom lines. However, they tempt us to forget that the creative process is just that—a process. John Kao, author of *Jamming: The Art & Discipline of Business Creativity*, defines creativity in business as, "the entire process by which ideas are generated, developed and transformed into value."[2] When we embrace the process, the product takes care of itself.

This book is about the *process* of living a creative life, a life of infinite possibility. Processes are more difficult to define than outcomes. Just as no one can define another's spiritual experience, neither can another tell us how to experience our creativity. Creativity will, of course, be experienced and expressed differently by everyone. While flexibility, joy, openness, and surprise-ability are all reflections of creativity, there is no one right way to achieve or experience them. This book is not intended to define a specific experience for the reader. That would be arrogant and disrespectful. It is meant to serve as a guide, to lead you back to what you once spontaneously and intuitively knew.

"Wait a minute!" you say. If we already have what we need to live wonderfully creative lives, why aren't we all doing it? Because of old misconceptions of creativity, that we are either born with it, or we're not. If we're not artistic, then we're not creative, and anyway, creative people are unstable, have difficulty holding down jobs, staying in relationships and pulling their weight in society. No wonder so many retreat to the safety of uncreative lives!

Most of us are socialized *out* of a healthy relationship to creativity, play, and wonder very early in life. We learn that having (or appearing to have) the "right" answer, fitting in, and getting peer approval is more important than trusting our own instincts. It is certainly more important than the risk of looking foolish. Educator Neil Postman said, "Children enter school as question marks and leave as periods."[3] We learn that the answer is more important than the question. Eventually we stop asking altogether.

We can use ideas from emerging holistic paradigms in physics, management and psychology, as well as the principles from theatrical improvisation to reignite our natural curiosity and become question marks again. We can break out of beliefs which have barred us from realizing our potential.

We can learn much to support us on our creative journey from the pioneers of the past century who broke through the limits of their own scientific paradigm to make discoveries about the subatomic world. Perhaps you feel that the sciences are forbidden territory, best left to those working long hours in secluded laboratories. We don't feel the same way about other fields—who needs a doctorate in political science to comment on the latest congressional bill? Who refrains from offering a review of the latest play, movie or concert because they didn't graduate from Julliard? Yet, if we are not scientists, we feel that we have little use for science and, perhaps, that it has little use for us.

In their book, *Science Matters: Achieving Scientific Literacy*, Robert Hazen and James Trefil make the point that *"doing* science is clearly distinct from *using* science."⁴ While doing science requires in-depth education and specialized expertise, using science asks only for an understanding of its principles. We all can understand and *use* the principles of science to illuminate our understanding of ourselves and our world—particularly the ground-breaking principles of the last century's exploration of the subatomic world. It would be inaccurate and misleading to say that the *same* phenomena are present in quantum physics as in the creative process. However, the subatomic world's unpredictable and dynamic nature has much to teach us (or more accurately, to *remind* us) about possibility in our lives.

The breakthrough discoveries of quantum physics set the stage for shifts in other fields, most notably in management and psychology. Quantum Creativity is a personal paradigm—a paradigm of possibility. Though I call it a personal paradigm, it is also a useful model for organizational transformation. I have had many opportunities to train organizations in these principles with powerful results.

Quantum Creativity allows us to tap into our deepest source. Ironically, this "new" paradigm is not so new to us at all, because it represents much of what we once knew as children. Nor is this perspective new in cultural history. Many non-Western spiritual traditions and native cultures are built on what we now herald as new age thinking.

Today, the word *quantum* has come to describe everything from alternative healing to computer software. Superficially, the word *quantum* suggests "new," "powerful," "extremely large," and "extremely small." There is some truth to these connotations, but while it is tempting to ride the tide of romance related to all things quantum, one could miss the significance of this profound scientific revolution. The discoveries of particle physics in the past century led scientists to a radical shift in the way they viewed the world and their relationship to it. This shift took scientists from a compartmentalized or mechanistic view of natural phenomena, to a holistic perspective. The world that quantum physicists describe is analogous to the world that artists, business people, children at play, teachers, and others experience when immersed in creative energy; it is an interconnected, participatory world, filled with infinite possibilities.

The principles that form the foundation of this new worldview apply far beyond the subatomic world they describe and help us understand our creative processes, as well as embrace life in the twenty-first century—a life which demands a commitment to a new paradigm for our survival and growth. The key principles of quantum physics can help us shift to a holistic, participatory, and intuitive relationship to life.

Chapter One lays the foundation for the principles of Quantum Creativity. Here, you will discover what the breakthroughs in several seemingly unrelated fields have in common. Each of the following chapters presents the principles that enabled such radical shifts in perception and shows you how to tap their power to unleash the possibilities in your life. The first section of these chapters begins with a description of the principle, often drawing parallels from the models in Chapter One.

The second section of each chapter is subtitled "Learned Blocks." Again, though we cannot be taught creativity, we *can* identify the blocks which have kept us from an abundant experience of our lives. Identifying these blocks is the first step toward unlearning them. It is the first step toward "Doing Things Differently"—the subtitle of the third section of each chapter.

The third section gives examples and ideas for practicing each principle. A person in a darkened room has little success in creating light by sitting in the dark, pondering the reasons for the darkness, the ramifications of continued darkness, and the impact darkness has had on his life. So, too, we will fail to rediscover life's possibilities if we lose ourselves in pondering and analyzing similar questions about creativity. The person in the darkened room simply needs to get up and turn on the light (or light a candle, or pull back the blinds, or turn on a flashlight). We simply need to do things differently to remove the darkness of creative blocks and to tap into our life energy.

Sometimes "Doing Things Differently" will suggest ways to restore our creative energy and innocence. It will also offer subprinciples and examples of how people from many backgrounds create possibilities by doing things differently. These examples and ideas are not a how-to guide to greater creativity. I do not believe there is a single prescription to cure what ails us—an idea that is itself mechanistic in nature. However, we can learn much from those who have gone before us. Their courage and wisdom inspire us as we find our own path.

Many of the Quantum Creativity principles contain aspects of the others. They have a holographic nature; just as each fragment of a hologram plate contains the information of the entire image[5], so do many of the principles of Quantum Creativity contain the wisdom of the entire paradigm.

While the principles are, by necessity, presented in a linear fashion, they are nonlinear in nature. Sometimes it is useful to follow them in the order I have set down and other times to follow another order altogether. More often than not, they take on a life of their own based on the present moment. Call them up as you need them. Live them, challenge them, explore them.

Maharishi Mahesh Yogi, one of my spiritual teachers, challenged his students not to believe anything he said until they found it to be true for themselves. He encouraged skepticism with participation. After all, how can we find out if something is true for us if we don't try it for ourselves? Therefore, paradigm shifting is a rigorous process—a participatory one. It is not simply an intellectual experience, but one that is also physical, emotional, and spiritual. Embrace this challenge. Open yourself up to the possibilities of the journey.

CHAPTER ONE

Quantum Creativity

4:56 a.m. I drag myself out of bed, gather a bag full of hand mirrors and smudge sticks and drive all over north Chicago to pick up ensemble members for the sunrise ritual. For months we have explored rituals from many cultures for a multi-media show. We now crave the first-hand experience outside our rented church basement rehearsal hall.

I ring doorbells in hushed neighborhoods and meet with squinting, groaning faces attached to equally reluctant bodies. Each silently joins me in the rusted-out Toyota station wagon I have borrowed for the drive to Lake Michigan's Fullerton Beach.

On this particular day the sun chooses not to participate, staying camouflaged behind thick clouds. We faithfully go through the motions of our "sun" ritual on the windy, chilly lake front—vigilantly relighting snuffed matches, pointing mirrors toward where the sun was supposed to be, and solemnly going through the paces of our cleansing ritual—each searching for the sacred in this ceremony we've created. After an hour of dedication to our spirits and the spirit of our developing show, we burst into peals of laughter at the futility of our efforts in the uncooperative weather conditions. We see the light; we head to our favorite greasy spoon for breakfast.

While it is difficult to pinpoint a specific line of dialogue or scene in the final production of *Rituals* that was influenced by our lakeside odyssey, our time together went a long way in building community, friendship and a sense of play in each of us. Play, discovery, trust, and community are the most valuable lessons I learn from evolving collaborative processes. They are the life blood of creativity and of living a creative life. Without them there can be little depth to any creative process.

My experience that early morning at Lake Michigan and many others like it remind me what I habitually forget about living a life of possibility, and it planted the seeds that ultimately grew into the principles of Quantum Creativity. Based on emerging paradigms in many fields including quantum physics, the principles of Quantum Creativity, as we shall see, represent the genius of nature in its ever-evolving creative process.

I became interested in the mysteries of the creative process when I began using theatrical improvisation as a tool to develop original theatre in the early 1980s. Although my theatre training was classical, I was consistently drawn to new, unformed work and demanding collaborative projects once I began my professional directing career.

As I used improvisation to flesh out new work and develop entirely original theatre, I saw several important by-products. Many of these were wonderfully beneficial to the final result, while others had little to do with it and were, as my friend Cheri would say, "icing on the gravy."

I and my fellow collaborating actors, designers, writers, composers, and choreographers would begin with a seed idea, a theme—even with our dreams. We then improvised, brainstormed and reflected on that idea in a workshop. Some of these sessions proved fiercely productive, while others left us groping in the dark. Regardless of the outward appearances of the workshop, it soon became clear to me that something was always germinating, even if it was hidden far beneath the surface.

As a group, we were building a creative community—an ensemble within which each person was a full participant and creative peer. Through successive collaborations we learned to trust the twists and turns of original work in process and, perhaps more important, to trust our intuition and subtlest impulses.

Fear was a regular visitor—fear of not knowing what was evolving, fear of failure, fear of losing control. Here I learned the definition of courage: fear meeting faith. I could feel afraid and forge ahead anyway. I learned to turn that fear over to the power of collective creativity, a far stronger force that easily dwarfed my occasional need to control or manipulate our work. Now our creative process could reach an even greater height—play.

Stephen Nachmanovich refers to this level as "galumph-ing" or as "the immaculately rambunctious and seemingly inexhaustible play-energy apparent in puppies, kittens, chil-dren, baby baboons—and also in young communities and civilizations."[6] Galumphing is exploration for its own sake. Play is valuing the process for the sake of the enjoyment it offers. Concern for the endpoint has no place here.

As a teacher and director of improvisation-based the-atre, I learned one of the most important lessons of my life—and one I need to remind myself of daily: the process *is* the product. Quantum Creativity, draws from my experience as a director and teacher and from the principles of theatrical improvisation, as well as of shared themes of recent discov-eries in physics, management, and psychology.

IMPROVISATION
From Spiritual To Spectacle

Most of us connect improvisation with comedy or jazz. These are notable descendants of a powerful tradition and age-old human impulse to channel a deeper creative spirit. Tracing this tradition (briefly) is valuable in learning more about our creative source.

The roots of theatrical improvisation can be traced to Shamanic traditions. The Shaman, or spiritual elder, of a tribe entered a trance and gave his or her body over as a "theatre for the gods."[7] The experience was transformative for both Shaman and congregation, although the Shaman often had no conscious memory of what transpired. Jesters, poets, and actors later became secular counterparts to the Shaman by channeling a deep creative spirit for audiences to share.[8]

Sixteenth century Italy saw the development of Commedia dell'arte theatre which included stock characters and scenarios or loosely developed plots within which the actors improvised. These improvisations often lampooned the news of the day or the most recent community scandal.[9]

In the United States, the late Viola Spolin is considered the mother of contemporary theatrical improvisation. Inspired by her teacher, Neva Boyd, she developed a series of games for children as part of a Works Progress Administration (WPA) program in the 1930s. She later expanded these games for use in the classroom and for training actors. Spolin's son, Paul Sills, grew up with these games and, as a student at the University of Chicago in the late 40s and early 50s, used them to develop topical original work in much the same way as his 16th century Italian predecessors did. His company, The Compass Players, spawned the formation of Second City in 1959.[10] Second City continues as a major force in the training of actors and a model for *Saturday Night Live*, as well as traditional and experimental improvisation troupes.

Throughout the ages improvisation has taught people to "respond to the immediate stimuli of the environment,"[11] and its early roots in spiritual traditions remain important today. To respond to the "immediate stimuli of the environment" we let go of the logic and control that often keeps us stuck and prevents us from noticing the subtle impulses of our creativity. Many of us are comfortable living out of our linear, rational left brain. Improvisation requires us to let go of rational understanding and practicality. It compels us to respond out of intuition and trust. Inspired in part by the power of improvisation, the principles of Quantum Creativity release us to infinite creative possibilities.

A PARADIGM EMERGES

Quantum Creativity is a personal paradigm—a worldview. Futurist Joel Arthur Barker says a paradigm "does two things: (1) it establishes or defines boundaries and (2) it tells [us] how to behave inside the boundaries in order to be successful."[12] Of course, this success is based on the expectations and limitations of the worldview itself.

A personal or organizational paradigm may be constructed out of our current values, culture, experiences, and objective understanding. It is easier for us to notice what is *different* from our experience, than to describe our current experience, especially if we do not have anything with which to compare our current experience. Try describing the characteristics that define your own culture, then try describing those of one very different from your own and you will see what I mean.

The paradigm within which we choose to operate (I believe we can, with increased awareness, *choose* our paradigm) has far-reaching implications. Indeed, some of us operate out of more than one, for example, choosing a different worldview in our personal lives than in our work lives. Our paradigm dictates how we perceive the world around us, how we interpret our experiences and all of the information we receive through our senses, intellect, intuition, and our spirituality.

For example, if I believe the world functions as a series of parts all operating independently of one another (as Decartes and Newton believed), I may not be concerned with what effect my actions have on those other parts (my fellow human beings, the environment, etc.). However, if I perceive the world as dynamic and interdependent, a living organism (as do many native cultures and holistic paradigms) I will be aware that any choice I make will influence the rest of the system, then I may consider my responsibility to the whole.

Just as the paradigm within which we choose to live determines our perceptions of the world, so, too, does it determine the range of possibilities before us. To recover a free-flowing relationship to our creativity, we must transform our personal paradigm, including our beliefs about the creative process. In subsequent chapters I discuss beliefs that prevent us from having an abundant relationship to this dynamic life energy and I offer principles and tools to help us reach the full potential of our creative selves.

We must replace these limiting beliefs about our creativity with new principles—a new paradigm, though one not really new to us at all. We all came into the world with a joyful, playful relationship to our creativity. Play was (and still can be) how we learned about ourselves and the world. Unfortunately over the years we learn to sacrifice these impulses in order to fit in.

Thus, creative release is more about remembering (literally, re-membering) what we once knew, than about learning something new. The quantum world is one of infinite potential, where there is only process—a world of mystery and creative energy. We will see that our very being has creative potential on the subatomic or quantum level of our existence. For that reason, I call this the paradigm of Quantum Creativity.

This book begins with an exploration of emerging models in physics, management, and psychology. These laid the foundation for principles of Quantum Creativity. That there are common threads between nature and the systems we have developed to function in the world is nothing short of inspiring. We can learn much from these connections. Nature, after all, is engaged in a perpetual creative process.

THE QUANTUM WORLDVIEW EVOLVES
From Mystical to Mechanical (and back again)

The mechanistic worldview is a recent development in world history. For thousands of years men and women experienced the mysteries of nature as integral—not only to each other, but to those who witnessed and, perhaps more important, participated in them. The mystical practices of the alchemists, the many cultures that worshipped goddesses, and the elaborate rituals of native peoples preparing for the hunt or celebrating the harvest are but a few examples. Many cultures struggle to retain this holism in the face of the overwhelming influence of modern society—a society that discounts these cultures as "primitive." This same mechanistic worldview has distanced its own members from the essentially holistic nature of the creative process, stifling our vision of possibilities.

The worldview developed in the seventeenth century which believed in knowing through repeatable and verifiable experimentation had resounding implications for the Western world. René Descartes boldly stated this new vision in his *Discourse on Method* in 1637. With Descartes' declaration and the ascendance of empiricism, the world was no longer seen as a living mystery, but as a vast machine, best understood if it was dismantled and reassembled and controlled by humans. We became objective observers of the world—a world now seen as separate from the observer; a world analyzed as independent parts and known on the basis of their behavior; a world under the scrutiny of the all-powerful scientist-observer.

Do not indict the scientific model itself here. Without it we would not enjoy much of the Western world's quality of life. I benefit from the scientific model this very moment as my computer stores my keystrokes as electronic data. When the mechanistic scientific model becomes a template for the experience and interpretation of *all* of life's processes it gives us the illusion that we are separate from the world and sets the stage for our current social and environmental turmoil. Hundreds of books now challenge the hegemony of this worldview, offering alternatives in a myriad of domains. From inquiries into physics, we can learn much about reestablishing sanctity in our relationship to the world. We can once again enjoy wonder and possibility as an everyday experience, rather than fine China reserved only for special occasions.

In the early 1800s physicists began to see limitations in Newton's laws of mechanics, as they studied the behavior of light. Newton held that light consisted of particles. Young's famous "double-slit" experiment in 1804 demonstrated the wave nature of light. Depending on the construct of the experiment, light behaved as a stream of particles (when light was able to pass through only one slit) or as waves (when both slits were open).[13] This paradoxical wave-particle duality was the first of many important discoveries that led to the development of quantum theory. In 1900, Max Planck's theory of black body radiation led him to propose that light was made up of discrete packages which he called quanta.[14] Quantum theory also exposed the limitations of many of the laws of Newtonian physics—laws which are effective in predicting the behavior of the macroscopic world, but fail when applied to the subatomic world.

Viewed through Newton's mechanistic paradigm, light should behave in only one way; and the expectations of the observer should not affect that measurement. The assumptions of classical physics are 1) the physical world can be known through measurement; and 2) objective observation is possible; that is, the act of measurement does not affect the phenomenon nor change the measurement. In contrast, the assumptions of quantum physics are 1) the physical world cannot be fully known through measurement because of randomness and unpredictability; and 2) it is impossible to observe anything in nature without disturbing it, because the observer and the observed are intimately connected.[15]

The lessons quantum physics teaches about creativity are already apparent. Creative life energy is filled with possibility; we cannot "observe" creativity without participating in it, nor can we experience it without changing it or ourselves. There are no objective observers—only participants who channel and transform creative energy. Just as in the double slit experiment, our expectations and beliefs about our creativity may well determine how that creativity manifests. Without expectations, our creativity is limitless.

Quantum theory is full of paradoxes that cannot be explained by the mechanistic paradigm. According to Heisenberg's Uncertainty Principle, it is impossible to measure both the momentum and location of electrons simultaneously. The phenomenon of the "quantum leap" also defies mechanistic logic. Electrons jump from one energy state to another—they simply cease to exist in one state, then re-appear in another.

Physicists can no longer think of the world strictly in terms of Newton's laws of mechanics or construe matter exclusively as a collection of independent subatomic particles. Subatomic particles are bundles of matter in constant vibration that seem to appear and disappear out of the dynamic quantum field. Fritjof Capra, physicist and author of *The Tao of Physics*, suggests that we think of particles as "processes rather than objects."[16]

By analogy, our attempts to analyze and control creativity can distort our perceptions and inhibit us from releasing our full potential. However, if we make a similar shift in our personal paradigm from mechanistic and objective to holistic and participatory, we access the profound possibilities of our creative resources.

Ultimately, the relationship between quantum physics and creativity surpasses analogy. The particles of quantum physics are literally the stuff of which we are made. An atom contains a dense nucleus and a thin cloud of spinning electrons. If you imagine an electric fan, the rotating blade seems to fill the entire doughnut-shaped volume it describes, but the blade actually occupies very little space. Just as the rapidly orbiting electrons seem to fill the atom, vibrating subatomic particles in our bodies give us the *experience* of solidity. Our physical reality is dynamic potential energy and can be our creative, spiritual, emotional, and intellectual reality as well.

Live in the quantum paradigm and the world becomes dynamic, interconnected, and participatory. It becomes a fertile environment for the creative in us and which we influence in return. We discover our interconnectedness. Living a creative life is not an objective process; we cannot separate ourselves from it or step back in observation. We must participate in our creative process or we will have none at all.

Creative expression is limited only by our ability to experience ourselves and our world. Realizing our full potential, then, has more to do with *getting out of the way* and *un*learning limiting beliefs than with learning anything new. Our creativity is there for us; we simply need to remember to be simple. Our lessons from quantum physics are profound; the universe is fundamentally holistic, participatory, observer-created, and based in potential energy. What fertile ground for creativity!

On the heels of the paradigm shift in physics are similar shifts in other fields. Many are changing from a mechanistic and objective paradigm to a holistic and participatory approach. I will highlight two such new paradigms, one in business and one in the psychology.

TOTAL QUALITY MANAGEMENT
Another Industrial Revolution

The word "paradigm" was made increasingly popular, as businesses explored new ways of working. The terms "paradigm," and "paradigm shift," however, often refer to superficial changes. A business may rearrange work stations and solve problems in teams without making a fundamental shift in the corporate culture. In other words, "If nothing changes, nothing changes." With all of the hoopla about responding to change, organizations rarely shift to a new cultural paradigm.

W. Edwards Deming developed one of the most significant management models, known as Total Quality Management, or TQM. Properly implemented, this model transforms organizational culture. Today organizations of all sizes routinely implement his paradigm-busting principles, such as continuous improvement and work teams.

Just as the scientists bumped up against the uncertainty of simultaneously measuring complementary quantities of objects, such as position and momentum, so too, did Deming realize the uncertainty of using only production quotas to measure business success. This shift from a sole reliance on quantitative measurements to inclusion of qualitative factors represents a shift toward a holistic appreciation of the production process.

Deming transformed the mechanistic approach to production into a collaborative approach to quality soon after Bohr and Heisenberg discovered the holistic nature of the subatomic world. Deming's work mirrors the new paradigm in physics. His approach is grounded in statistics, as are the probability equations of quantum physics. TQM also employs key principles that support creativity.

"Continuous Improvement" is one of Deming's central ideas.[17] A company cannot simply improve its production line or marketing strategy and then sit back and relax. TQM requires continuous improvement in all areas at all times. To achieve this, individuals in the organization must be empowered to make improvements in their own areas.

Deming's "Continuous Improvement" is key to creative success. Making discoveries (discussed in detail in Chapter Nine), engaging wonder and the willingness to be surprised all open the doors to our creative process. Maintaining a questioning attitude is as important to success in business as it is for success in life.

Another of Deming's principles is "Drive out Fear."[18] He noticed that many workers were so afraid of losing their jobs due to a mistake, that they were reluctant to present their ideas to improve operations. Fear stifles people and stops them from exploring solutions or making improvements. Deming's philosophy promotes fearlessness and organizational cultures that are fertile grounds for creativity and innovation. In my discussion of improvisation, I referred to fear as one of the biggest blocks to individual and collective creativity. Deming acknowledged this when he made "Drive Out Fear" one of his key principles.

After its initial war-time success, Deming's ideas met with surprising resistance in the United States. The subsequent acceptance of TQM represents a radical paradigm shift in American industry. In recent years other visionaries have built on Deming's work to help businesses break through self-imposed limitations. Peter Senge *(The Fifth Discipline)*, Tom Peters *(Thriving on Chaos)*, and Margaret Wheatly *(Leadership and the New Science)* are a few such notables. Each of their approaches identifies the limitations of the mechanistic paradigm and advocates holistic and participatory organizational models.

For such an organizational transformation to be successful, however, new paradigm principles must be accepted and owned by each individual in the organization. I regularly hear reports from employees of companies involved in new management initiatives designed to improve productivity, innovation, and teamwork. Shifting paradigms in business runs deeper than re-arranging work stations and holding team meetings. While promising, such endeavors are often sabotaged by key players who keep one foot firmly planted in the old paradigm. Nothing is more damaging to morale than management advocating change, but being unwilling to let go of the control necessary to allow it to happen. Each individual must become reacquainted with the joy of participation and encouraged to risk being "out of control."

THE RECOVERY MODEL
Healing the Whole Person

As was true in other fields, psychology's pioneers operated out of an essentially mechanistic paradigm. Freud's theory of the id, ego, and superego laid the foundation for further compartmentalization of the psyche. Through analysis, psychoanalysts believe, the problem can be identified and a treatment plan implemented. This model assumes a clear cause and effect relationship between past experience and present behavior. Once this relationship is understood by both patient and therapist, control is regained and with it relief from suffering occurs. The defective part is isolated from the system so it can be repaired to get the system up and running again.

The emphasis on restoring the person to a state where he can function again in the environment begs challenge. Perhaps the environment itself is part of the problem, e.g. an abusive family setting, a dysfunctional or inappropriate work environment and/or a social circle that does not support growth. Perhaps the feelings (depression, rage, grief, etc.) that brought the individual to seek help are an important doorway to healing—not to be seen as a problem to be solved (read, "medicated" or "figured out") but an opportunity to move through to a deeper level of self-knowledge—an opportunity to integrate mind, body, and spirit.

A new paradigm has evolved in response to the limitations of the mechanistic approach of the psychotherapeutic model. Its seeds were planted in the desperation of severely progressed alcoholics who sought every means available (treatment programs, shock therapy, analysis, and even incarceration) to overcome their craving for the drug that was destroying their lives. Not until the problem was viewed from a spiritual perspective through the birth of Alcoholics Anonymous in 1935 did those suffering from alcoholism identify it as a disease and begin to find lasting relief and hope.[19]

Alcoholics Anonymous, and the countless 12-step programs it has spawned, centers on an admission of powerlessness over addiction (an understanding that it takes more than "will power" to overcome the addiction), faith in a power greater than oneself (the addict must let go of control and ask for help outside of herself if recovery is to begin);

and the fellowship of the group (recovering addicts offer "experience, strength and hope" to each other). Another important contribution of the AA model is the acceptance of recovery as process. You will not hear recovering addicts talking about themselves as "cured." The focus is on the process, not the product—a key creativity principle as well.

The grass roots success of the 12-step model laid the foundation for an approach previously thought to be the sole domain of psychologists and psychiatrists. Anne Wilson Schaef, Ph.D., a psychotherapist by training, developed Living Process work, an alternative to therapy based on healing the whole person. Living Process work rejects the notion of an objective observer/therapist, instead the individual is a full participant in the recovery process. In this system, each individual has the tools and knowledge to heal.

Schaef and others (Peter Breggin, Christina and Stanislav Grof, Chellis Glendenning, Ron Kurtz, Jaqueline Small, and Donald Epstein, to name a few) challenge the mechanistic approach to healing in their work and writings.

Schaef defines the addictive process as that which "keeps us unaware of what is going on inside us"[20] or from "knowing what we know and feeling what we feel."[21] We must first begin to recover from our addictions before we can become fully available to "feel what we feel and know what we know." We cannot be in direct relationship to our creative process if we distract ourselves from our deeper source.

The recovery model holds that addiction is primarily a spiritual disease. The connection between addiction and spirituality is nothing new. Many spiritual traditions focus on attachment and desire as the primary obstacles to a relationship with God and/or a spiritual life.

The connection is clear. If we are distracted by our attachments, we cannot be available to the quiet impulses of our creative process. Stephen Nachmanovich says that, "Improvisation is intuition in action."[22] We might also say that creativity is *spirituality* in action. If we are cut off from one, our experience of the other will be greatly diminished. When we become more available to one, our availability and enjoyment of the other increases.

Each of these emerging paradigms (improvisation, quantum physics, TQM, and the recovery model) shares principles with the others and a common foundation in a field of all possibilities: improvisation leads to infinite creative potential; quantum physics is based in the dynamic quantum field; Total Quality Management has an unbounded commitment to innovation and continuous improvement; and the recovery model draws on the many-layered mysteries of spirituality. These paradigms can light the way for a life that is inherently holistic, participatory, and overflowing with infinite possibility.

Creativity can flourish in businesses, church basements, windy beaches, work stations, concert halls, team meetings, living rooms, classrooms, artists' lofts, and wherever creative spirits eagerly welcome the mystery of life.

CHAPTER TWO

Listen to Your Essence

After weeks of frustration circling the streets in his new city neighborhood in search of parking, Ramón tries a new method. He pulls over or takes a quiet moment at a stoplight and "listens" for directions to the next open parking space. The directions inevitably come when he asks. "Turn right at the next block." "Pull into the alley and head back where you came from." Or, "Just pull over and wait a few minutes; someone is about to pull out." In the last several months he reports his intuition or, as he calls it, The Parking Goddess, Asphaltia, led him to open spots nine out of ten times!

THE PRINCIPLE

LISTEN TO YOUR ESSENCE is a direct challenge to a mechanistic way of being. In a world perceived as a machine, the concepts of Essence, intuition, hunches, and gut feelings have little value. This principle *demands* integration of mind, body, and spirit.

Before we can listen to our Essence, we must know one exists—that core which is essentially us and, perhaps, essentially universal. Some describe it as intuition or an inner voice, while others experience it spiritually, naming it higher power or God.

Here are a few of the ways my students and workshop participants describe their experience of Essence:

> *Essence is [an] internal deep voice of wisdom. It*
> *is an internal compass that gives us direction. It*
> *is extremely important to have a strong and con-*
> *stant relationship with our Essence in order not*
> *to lose sight of who we are.*
>
> —JEFF TWOREK

> *Essence is constantly changing and evolving...*
> *it is dynamic. In fact, it is the core dynamic that*
> *makes me me. And just about the time I think*
> *I've put my finger on it, it shifts or transforms*
> *into something else. It is the invisible thing that I*
> *follow by watching for it between—between*
> *thought, between feelings, between anything you*
> *can identify as "is" or having a quality of solidity*
> *on any level. It is what delights the heart. It is the*
> *mystical self that sets my foot on the right path*
> *and the source of knowledge of what is right for*
> *me in every sense.*
>
> —PAULA LUEDTKE

*Essence is mostly spiritual. It is an inner voice
that guides me when I ask it to. I also think that
my Essence is stronger in my sleep and comes
through during my dreams. Sometimes if I go to
bed thinking of a problem, I dream about it and
wake up with an answer.*

–LORI DOLL

*Essence [is] a kindling fire, embers burning at the
core of my existence. It is the source of all that is
good about me–intellectually, emotionally, cre-
atively. Another word for it might be "potential."
It has definite spiritual connections for me and
when I am in touch with whatever is going on
with my Essence, I feel closer to God. Perhaps it is
the incarnation of the God-like within me.*

–CYNTHIA NORRIS

Perhaps these descriptions will remind you that you
know more about your Essence than you thought.
Language always limits us in describing the mysterious, illusive, or spiritual. Any words we try to put to that which is
essentially us, and yet much greater than us, limits the limitless. Only because the form of this book is necessarily one
of language, must I find words to communicate that which
is essentially unnamable. I refer to the experience primarily
as "Essence" and occasionally as "intuition" or "higher
power." I do not intend for these words to define any single
experience, but to communicate the possibilities of experience.

Some believe that Essence or a higher power must be
mystical and sensational–something very unlike day-to-day
experiences. This dramatization of spirituality can cut us off
from what is right in front of us–from what we already
know.

We strive for something that is already there. We do not need to work at being spiritual. In the same way, we do not need to work at being creative. We *are* creative beings. We came into the world this way. To let go of what cuts us off from a clear, consistent relationship with our creative spirit is getting out of the way. This is listening.

When we have difficulty listening to our Essence, it's possible that we have forgotten the true nature of listening. Most of us think we are good listeners, although, more often than not, when we think we are listening, we are busy with our thoughts and composing our responses. We are busy talking (usually in our heads) when we should be listening. I have often heard people describe "prayer" as asking for help, and "meditation" as listening for the answer. Many of us forget the listening part.

In my communication and collaboration workshops, I start by teaching listening skills. Listening serves as the foundation for all types of communication, even communication with ourselves! If we are not available to clearly receive incoming information, we certainly cannot make good use of the information we *do* hear. Inaccurate or distorted information is useless at best and dangerous at worst. We begin relationships that aren't right for us, take unrewarding jobs, make purchases we later regret—all because we are unwilling, or unable, to practice LISTEN TO YOUR ESSENCE.

When we first practice listening, it is not unusual to "hear" nothing or to experience only the chatter of our frenetic thoughts. "My elbow itches. . . I think I've put on a few pounds this month...I need to make a dentist appointment...I wonder if that card I sent for Mother's Day is too sappy...." And we're off! Have faith. Building a relationship with your Essence is a process and, like all relationships, it needs regular attention to grow.

The subatomic world is analogous to Essence. Electrons may occupy only certain levels of energy. Electrons naturally go into the lowest available energy level or state of least excitation, but the lowest energy levels can accommodate the fewest electrons, so some electrons must occupy higher energy levels.[23] In the same way we, too, gravitate towards our Essence when we allow ourselves to be without distraction. Our ground state is the source of infinite power and creative potential.

The more we know about the world of subatomic particles, the more we see our spirituality reflected therein. As stated earlier, scientists now know that most of the volume of the atom is empty (matter is concentrated in the nucleus) and that subatomic particles behave as both waves and particles. In quantum field theory, the field from which these particle-wave-energy impulses spring (and to which they return) is considered anything but empty—at least not in the way we have come to think of emptiness. It is a dynamic field, a field of all possibilities, a field of infinite creative potential. The essence of matter has the same range of possibilities as the essence of our being, the essence of our creative spirit. All too often we miss this connection because we have been taught to think of mind and matter as separate.

If we draw an analogy between the quantum field and Essence, we cannot separate our physical selves and our creative process from our Essence. A mechanistic culture encourages us to dismember body from spirit. For centuries Eastern philosophers have called this separation an illusion. The death of our creative self is brought on by living this illusion.

When we allow ourselves the time and space to experience the essential level of our being, we are often surprised at how much we *do* know about ourselves and what we need and want from life. Like the dynamic quantum field, our Essence is anything but empty. It is the source of all our thoughts, intuitions, and passions—of infinite energy and possibilities.

Artists, parents, teachers, and healers have long relied on a connection with Essence to meet the moment-to-moment challenges in their work. They start with a plan or a vision knowing that they need to be willing to throw that plan out at any moment in response to a new discovery. Those unavailable to their Essence struggle to keep their "plan" intact or to maintain an illusion of control for control's sake, rather than honor the mischievous, unpredictable creative process that is life.

In recent years intuition has emerged from the arts, mysticism, and what once was considered the proprietary domain of women. "Essential Wisdom" plays a significant role in everything from new product development to hiring decisions. Companies such as AT&T, PepsiCo and Aetna now offer introspection and reflection training to their management executives. Edward McCraken, CEO of Silicon Graphics, says:

> *"The most important trait of a good leader is knowing who you are. In our industry very often we don't have time to think. You have to do all your homework, but then you have to go with your intuition without letting your mind get in the way."*[24]

Practicing the principle of LISTEN TO YOUR ESSENCE can reveal a wealth of information, whether it is the "hunch" we follow in business, the subtle whispers which lead us to our purpose in life, the apparent whims which give us important new information about ourselves or, most important of all, a chance to enjoy *being* in our simplest state—the state of silent awareness that is true intimacy with ourselves and the universe. Unfortunately, the riches of our Essence are not always readily available to us because along the way we picked up a few:

LEARNED BLOCKS

Learned Blocks are the powerful messages that cut us off from seeing life's possibilities. Insidious and often unconscious, the worldview we construct out of these myths is solid, but not invincible. Once we identify these blocks we can let go of them and do things differently.

We learned to **SECOND-GUESS OUR INTUITION**. We mistrust anything that is not concrete, practical, or verifiable. Whether we sit on an idea in a problem-solving session at work without sharing it or go against our better judgment by doing something contrary to our gut wisdom, we devalue the messages of our Essence.

We all have stories of things going badly when we didn't trust our intuition. Recently I was invited to celebrate a friend's birthday. She had the wonderful idea to invite all of her female friends to a Japanese spa to soak and steam, then join her in the restaurant adjacent to the spa for sushi. As the day approached I felt less like going to the spa portion of the evening and thought maybe I should just meet up with the group at the restaurant.

It wasn't like me to want to miss an opportunity to soak in a hot tub, so I wrote off my resistance to midwinter fuddy-duddyness, had a light snack to hold me until our late dinner, and drove to the spa. Once in the steam room, I was enjoying a conversation with a friend I hadn't seen for months, when I started feeling light headed. I soon excused myself to the locker room to cool off. Before I knew it I was staring up at a circle of friends and recovering from a bad bump on the head after passing out. Later, my doctor insisted I visit the emergency room to be checked out. Because I didn't take my intuition seriously, that ended up being the most expensive birthday party I'd ever attended. Unfortunately, sometimes the consequences of not practicing LISTEN TO YOUR ESSENCE are much more severe than a bad headache and an unexpected medical bill!

Try as we might to do the "right" thing, sometimes we even get in trouble when we **LISTEN TO AUTHORITIES**. There is nothing inherently wrong with listening to authorities. It is one way to find guidance as we face challenges in our lives. It becomes a *block* when we give our power away to these authorities without checking in with our Essence—the ultimate authority. We get caught up in the "shoulds" of society or expectations of peers and family, just like the townspeople who oooohed and ahhhed as the emperor proudly walked naked down the street in his "new clothes." It becomes more important to meet the expectations of authorities than to risk rocking the boat by following the wisdom of our Essence.

From the time she was a little girl, Michele, an artist and designer, loved to paint and draw. As a child she received many awards for her work. Her mother told her, "You are going to be an artist, just like me. Look at your hands; you have my hands." While Michele's parents were more supportive of creative expression than most, they counseled her not to "waste time" on art for art's sake, but to concentrate on a career as a commercial artist. Despite her passion for fine art, she followed her parents directions and enrolled in a commercial art program. Upon completion she landed her first entry-level job in a large ad agency in Chicago.

Michele spent years moving up the corporate ladder and was an award-winning art director, when she realized she could no longer be a slave to others' expectations. She felt motivated more by awards and attention, than by her inner longing. The stress had taken its physical, emotional, and spiritual toll, too. Eventually, Michele needed to go "cold turkey" and withdraw from this spirit-killing experience. In her R & R time, she listened to her Essence.

Today, twenty years after she began this journey, Michele has reconnected to her Essence and is listening to it. She has returned to art school to study her first love, fine arts. Her lost passion is found.

It takes some of us longer to find our passion than others because we are caught up in **BUSY-NESS**. Busy-ness is the drug of choice for many—and why not? We tell ourselves that we're too busy for creativity. There are so many things to do: the closets need to be cleaned out, bills have to be paid, the dog needs her teeth cleaned, and before we know it, we don't even need to bother with those nasty nagging feelings.

Les has worked in social services most of his life. Each day presents hundreds of opportunities to focus on other people's needs and on innumerable projects.

> *I found that I was spending so much time focusing outside of myself, that when I needed to know what I was feeling, I couldn't. There are other times when I know I was using my busy-ness to avoid things I just didn't want to deal with. I still do sometimes. It's a hard habit to break.*

How many times have well-meaning friends advised us to "just keep busy" when we experience difficult periods in our lives? Busyness *is* an effective way to numb feelings. Feelings, nonetheless, are a lifeline back to our Essence. When we cut that line, it's hard to find our way back. Unfortunately, we can get used to this disconnection and don't hear the news flashes from our Essence when we need them. This may be the wake up call we need to start:

DOING THINGS DIFFERENTLY

Shifting paradigms is not accomplished through intellectual understanding alone, but by also *doing* things differently. Here are a few ideas:

MAKE TIME TO LISTEN. Milton's familiar line, "They also serve who only stand and wait"[25] reminds us of the value of doing nothing or what may *appear* to be nothing. Yogis who spend much of their lives in meditation, monks and others who take vows of silence teach us the value of taking time to listen—of simply *being* for the sake of being. I have often wondered if these gentle, unassuming souls are the ones who truly keep the world from spinning off its axis—not the movers and shakers to whom we give so much of our power in Western culture.

We can acquire the habit of listening even when we don't think we need information. Like the CEO who leaves her door open, thereby announcing her availability to have people stop in, share new information, and air concerns. She knows that every time she opens the door she will not be flooded with a line of employees eager to provide new insights *and* by establishing the routine of an open door, she knows these insights will come when they are ready.

We can establish the same "open door policy" with our Essence—our source of inspiration and insight. If we take time to connect with our deeper power only when in crisis or faced with a major decision, we may well find that the line has been disconnected or that there is so much mind-chatter that we cannot decipher the message. When we make time to listen as a regular part of our day, the line stays open and the connection is often clear.

When we make time to listen we can also **REMEMBER TO BREATHE**. Zen practice encourages us to be mindful of our experience of ourselves. This can be done simply by bringing attention to our breathing. Tension or deep emotions tempt us to hold our breath, perhaps out of fear or a need to control. Our breath takes us to our center, to our Essence. When we hold it, we cannot get there.

William Hanrahan, a voice teacher and communication consultant, has taught people how to reconnect to their true voice through conscious breathing for more than 20 years. He shared his experience working with a woman challenged by the process of conscious breathing.

> *I said to her, 'You know you are breathing as if there isn't enough. You are trying to hang on to the breath that you've got.' She said, 'Oh, my God! That's how I treat the rest of my life! There's never enough time, there's never enough money, there's never enough men—there's just never enough!' So breath, for her, became a metaphor for opening up other areas of her life.*[26]

Breath, then, is more than a metaphor for life, it *is* life. When we let go of our breath and drink it in as the infinite resource it is, we let life in. Breathe as you live. Live as you breathe. With each breath comes an opportunity to do things differently, to make a new choice.

Of breathing writer, Anne Lamott, shares:

> *This is not something I remember to do very often, and I do not normally like to hang around people who talk about slow conscious breathing; I start to worry that a nice long discussion of aroma therapy is right around the corner. But these slow conscious breathers are on to something, because if you try to follow your breath for a while, it will ground you in relative silence.*[27]

"Relative silence" leads us to **BE SIMPLE**. A friend confided her struggle to connect with her Essence. "I'm trying to listen, but the crazy voices are so much louder than my inner voice!" How many times have we struggled to separate our "crazy voices" from the voice of our Essence. Busyness, fear and urgency are only a few distractions that can cloud our perception and distort our understanding of the Essential message.

Hans Hoffman said, "The ability to simplify means to eliminate the unnecessary so that the necessary can speak." [28] To be simple is to come back to center and ask what is necessary there. In our quest for perfection we try too hard. When we stay simple, we are often surprised to find we already own what we seek. Sometimes the answer does not come right away. In time we discover it. Just as with our search for the elusive parking space, we will be led, if we take time to listen.

CHAPTER THREE

Follow Your Passion

Angela enjoyed a thriving career as a professional actress in regional theatre for more than fifteen years. She made her living exclusively through work in legitimate theatre—a rare occurrence, especially outside of New York. Ever since she was a little girl she dreamed of becoming an actress, and she made her every life choice based on that goal.

In the midst of her success, Angela began to get a nagging feeling that she would not be doing what she was doing much longer. She remembers feeling angry, even duped—"that wasn't part of the bargain! After all, I'd had a plan!"

She lived and worked with this discomfort for a year. She grew to accept that she needed to let go of what had been the focus of her life energy, though she had no idea what was next. Angela describes it as the "first time I had nothing to pin my identity on—no external means of identifying myself." At the end of that year, and still in the midst of "not knowing what's next," the thought came to Angela: "Maybe I should see a therapist." Just as she was considering this possibility, a second thought came to her: "You should BE a therapist." She had discovered her "what's next."

Angela sat with this quiet knowing for some months until a road trip back to her home town in Oregon with her best friend from graduate school. Even with this most trusted friend, she feared naming this new dream. When she eventually did, Rachel responded, "Of course! That's perfect! You'll be a wonderful therapist!" A few miles further they drove through a double rainbow—the universe's blessing was not lost on them. When Angela told her parents of her rumblings, they cheered. From that point on she never wavered from her new path.

Certainly there were obstacles along the way, but Angela shared, "I now know that the perceived problems are part of the path—and they do take care of themselves. When I am off-center, I think they are there to thwart me, when, in fact, they are part of the path, and moving through them propels me forward."

THE PRINCIPLE

Angela knew that it is difficult to be creative or gain a new perspective without passion. She had the patience to allow her new passion to emerge and does not regret the time she allowed herself. Corporations spend millions of training dollars each year teaching idea-generation and problem-solving techniques and are surprised when results are minimal. It's really no surprise. Think about a task you least like to do, be it washing dishes, filing, returning calls, any number of things. How often are you inspired to be creative in the midst of activities that give you no joy?

It is possible to find enjoyment in even the most mundane tasks. First, we must find some connection or personal meaning. We are tapped into our Essence passionately when even the envelope stuffing, toilet cleaning, and filing aspects of our work give us pleasure. When in tune with our passion we are energized by participation. Practicing someone *else's* passion, often leaves us drained.

Business is beginning to support passion in the workplace. W. Edwards Deming said, "Our prevailing system of management has destroyed our people."[29] He meant hierarchical management models focused on meeting *others'* expectations and, above all, on never making mistakes. Peter Senge's model of the "learning organization" is an effective antidote to the fear and apathy engendered by the old system. Senge's model helps workers rediscover passion and the innate desire to learn and grow. One of the most important ways we learn is by making mistakes and following our passion. When it is drained from us or replaced with someone else's, we begin to die inside.

Without passion, we easily step outside our integrity, abandoning our moral center. We may start "accidentally" taking home a few office supplies, making excessive personal calls from work, perhaps fudging an expense report, or engaging in potentially damaging gossip. We don't need the church, a personnel policy, or boss to tell us when we have compromised our integrity; if we check in with ourselves, more often than not our own moral barometer will tell us.

Without passion we simply do not care. *With* passion we feel ownership and a willingness to assume risk. In fact, we may not even feel we are taking risks because we are being guided by something much more powerful than ourselves. Isn't this how being in love feels? Perhaps this is why Matthew Fox counsels us to "fall in love at least three times a day."[30] When we are in love we are unstoppable.

There are many ways to fall in love. Passion is as necessary for a successful business negotiation as it is for creating or performing a symphony. In *A Passion for Excellence*, Tom Peters and Nancy Austin write about the necessity of this life energy in organizations, "And Passion it is. Topflight performance is not dry or deadly; it is spirited and emotion-filled."[31]

Conductor and composer Lukas Foss deems love the essential motivation to create. "If one uses music that one does not really love, then one will not succeed in making it one's own."[32] There is no ownership without passion, no connection to Essence and, thus, no creativity. Robert Bone, Professor of Law at Boston University, encourages students in a similar manner:

> *Steep yourself in the literature and the law you*
> *really want to do. If you become intimately*
> *familiar with it, enough to understand the deep*
> *level of what's going on...then new ideas will just*
> *come to you.[33]*

Individual and collaborative creativity is fueled by passion—an excitement for discovery and an insatiable capacity to be surprised. Most of us have had the experience that Professor Bone describes. As we practice FOLLOW YOUR PASSION, ideas and inspiration flood in. Suddenly the world rallies in support, and we run into the perfect contact at our spouse's office picnic (the event we craftily tried to miss). Perhaps a friend sends an article our way with a note saying, "Thought you might be interested in this!" and it turns out to release an insight that was the missing piece for our proposal; or we flip channels on a rainy Sunday afternoon only to discover a documentary on our favorite subject.

FOLLOW YOUR PASSION can also be like following a trail of bread crumbs. We may not know where it leads us or whether it's a trail at all. Sometimes the first "crumb" appears to us as an "aha!" like Angela's knowing, "I'm going to be a therapist!" At other times, we simply feel a heightened engagement with life at each step along the bread crumb trail, and where it leads seems irrelevant.

FOLLOW YOUR PASSION grows directly out of the first principle of LISTEN TO YOUR ESSENCE. We certainly cannot follow passion without knowing our Essence, for Essence leads us to passion. The word "enthusiasm" is a synonym for passion and comes from the Greek "enthousiasmos" or "entheos," "filled will God" or spirit.

Practicing LISTEN TO YOUR ESSENCE opens the door for spirit to fill us, to enthuse us. We then need to become willing to act on these intuitions, the sometimes "still small voices," whispering in quiet moments or when we least expect them. Theatre director, Mary Zimmerman, says, "The only difference between a creative person and an uncreative person is that a creative person takes her ideas seriously." To

QUANTUM CREATIVITY

54

take our ideas seriously we need to trust their source and
let go of control.

Sue Whitaker, a social worker, describes her experience:

> *Losing myself is how I know passion.... Passion is*
> *the voice of my soul. My ego, expressed as person-*
> *ality, hates my passion, finding it to be disorderly*
> *and unpredictable. I value passion as the spark*
> *that ignites my channel to God.*

Linna Tucker began pursuing dance years after many
dance professionals would have looked for less demanding
work.

> *I feel fortunate. I know so many people who have*
> *given up their passions and go through life with*
> *no joy. I feel sorry for people who give up fight-*
> *ing for their purpose.... We must have courage*
> *and, in the face of criticism and distractions,*
> *express our Godselves. It's not a choice, but an*
> *obligation to our spirits and the well-being of the*
> *planet.*

Like Linna, many people I interviewed for this book
about the role of passion in their lives spoke in spiritual
terms. They experience a *responsibility* to live a creative life,
not only for their own welfare, but for the health of their
families, community, and planet. This is the Hindu the idea
of dharma—that each of us has a path to fulfillment. We can
find it only through listening to our Essence and following
our passion.

There is a distinction between "quick fix" and Essential
passions. FOLLOW YOUR PASSION is not about transitory
whims or attractions that may harm us and distract us from
our journey (unhealthy relationships, excessive TV, over-

work, and acquiring newer and shinier possessions, to name only a few). These attractions, or more appropriately labeled, *compulsions*, are not rooted in our Essence. They are not filled with the life force. Unfortunately, we are sometimes deceived by our initial rush of excitement and adrenaline to believe that these false passions are the real thing.

In his book, *The Universe is a Green Dragon*, physicist Brian Swimme explores the power of passion in Nature herself. He notices parallels between the sun's attraction to the earth, an electron's attraction to the nucleus, and human attractions, be they to gardening, Shakespeare, another person, exercise, or a myriad of other expressions of life energy.

> *We awake to our own unique sets of attractions. So do oxygen atoms. So do protons. The proton is attracted only to certain particles. On an infinitely more complex level, the same holds true for humans: Each person discovers a field of allurements, the totality of which bears the unique stamp of that person's personality. Destiny unfolds in the pursuit of individual fascinations and interests.... By pursuing your allurements, you help bind the universe together. The unity of the world rests on the pursuit of passion.* [34]

Of course, none of us is in touch with our passion at every moment of our lives, and passion may express itself in rather mundane ways. I have gone through long periods in which I felt no clear sense of passion for any endeavor. These are not depressions, but simply times when I do my work, enjoy my friends and family, and simultaneously ask, "What's next? What is the next wave which will carry my creative spirit?" I call these my sensory deprivation periods, times when I listen to my Essence and get back silence.

These periods are part of the ebb and flow of living a creative life. They are crucial, just as slow cooking is crucial to some wonderful meals. As with the slow-cooked meal, something *is* happening—just not something I see or experience. My passion eventually does rise to the top of my creative crock pot and I am ready to embrace it (something I could not have done had it revealed itself any earlier).

Some of us are hindered in practicing FOLLOW YOUR PASSION with open-armed abandon, because of our:

LEARNED BLOCKS

We cut ourselves off from passion in much the same way we cut ourselves off from Essence, with busy-ness, distraction, and second guessing. At these times we faithfully did our best to **KEEP OUR ENTHUSIASUM IN CHECK**. To get excited is to risk ridicule. Passion is messy, loud, and non-linear—a threat to others desperately trying to keep their own in check.

Sam learned early in life to hide his passion. When he delighted in collecting butterflies, he was ridiculed by his older brother and classmates. He loved to read, but had to find secret places to do so, in order not to risk being thought of as different. As he grew older, he dealt with fear of others' opinions by becoming apathetic about his passions.

"It was just safer that way," he shared. "I decided I'd rather not be thought of as weird and I certainly wasn't willing to risk losing the approval of my brother, whom I idolized."

Sometimes we are more comfortable with people in crisis or great pain than with people experiencing joy and passion. We tell our enthusiastic friends we are happy for them, and secretly feel relieved when they return their attention to life's mundane challenges and disappointments.

If we do not follow our own passion, the passion of others can actually be painful to be around. And, if we spend much time around others who are not following their passion, keeping ours in check is reinforced. We may even ridicule those cracking open the door to let their spirit rush in and enthuse them. It is said that if we are not part of the solution, we are part of the problem. When we do not practice FOLLOW YOUR PASSION we become part of the problem. Here we discovered **SHAME**.

Shame is a learned response based on a distorted belief system, on the mythology of "shoulds." When we think we *should* make more money; we *should* be over that loss; we *should* have finished school, we *should* have more, do more, be more; we are swept up in the funnel cloud of shame. It lifts us off our center, spins us around and flings us far off course. Rooted in internalizing others' expectations or imagined social authority, shame dictates what is "right," and, more important, what is "wrong."

Shame blocks us from knowing our passion and needs in ways large and small. I was at a spiritual retreat in a beautiful wooded area some years ago. A small lake, hiking trails, horses, and various other outdoor adventures beckoned. I love the outdoors and am often the first one to jump in whenever there is a body of water nearby. This retreat was different, however. I only wanted to sleep. Despite my mysterious exhaustion, I dragged myself to the meetings and meals and made a valiant attempt at socializing. At one session I shared my frustration with my fatigue and struggle to participate fully. After a silence, the workshop leader gently responded, "What would happen if you slept as much as you needed?"

What an idea! I was so caught up in participating the "right" way, that it had not occurred to me to listen to my body and rest as much as I needed. (I now realize the irony here; at a spiritual retreat, I was ignoring the voice of my spirit!) Ever since, I have found many opportunities to ask versions of the workshop leader's question. What would happen if I registered for that sign language class, took those sailing lessons, went on that road trip out West, started that short story? In other words, what would happen if I *listened* to my Essence and *followed* my passion? Could I be stalled by another learned block? **BE PRACTICAL.**

Inspiration often comes in odd packages. This can be a bit scary. Most of us would like to know the outcome of our actions in advance—that's only practical, right? Not only is it not practical, it's not possible—and it's certainly not creative living.

As an undergraduate theatre student, I focused intense energy on building experience and skills as a stage manager (one who oversees the needs of production, rehearsals and performance). I thought that was "practical." I would have marketable skills and a list of professional credits to my name when I graduated. There was one hitch, summed up best by a T-shirt I recently saw which read: "What I really want to do is direct."

I, however, chose to direct on the sly, directing late-night shows with intern companies at regional theatres and watching other directors work. To be sure, this was a wonderful education for a young director. However, as the years passed, I found myself stifled by others' perceptions of me, and (even more debilitating) by my *self*-perception.

I came to think of myself as a "production person," not as an artist. This self-view was deadly to my creative spirit. How we perceive ourselves has a powerful effect on how much of our creativity we express. It wasn't until I weaned myself from the "practical" work that paid my rent for a number of years and put all of my energy into directing that I began to recover my full creative self and restored the possibilities.

Ben Hollis, a TV producer and musician, went through a similar work experience. He calls it the "professionalisation" of his creative process. "As soon as I got a new idea," he told me, "the wheels would start to turn and I would begin to think, 'How can I market this? How will I be able to make money off of this?'" Those impulses lurk beneath the surface for most creatives; we try to make sense of the process or decide on the viability of our ideas well before we give them a chance to take shape.

There are *many* ways to FOLLOW YOUR PASSION and still keep a roof over our heads. Angela's experience testifies to this. The universe loves to support those who live to their full potential and pursue dreams. It asks only that we trust that we will be taken care of, even when we cannot imagine how. This is a challenge if we also learned **DON'T TAKE RISKS**.

As "be practical's" partner in crime, this block tells us that anything that takes us into the unknown is dangerous and perhaps fatal. Little support exists for risk-taking—letting go of something we have in order to get something we want. Emotional, physical, and spiritual risks bring with them the possibility of loss. Sometimes we risk losing something without which we are convinced we cannot live.

Some years ago I obsessed over owning a Ford Explorer. I spent months shopping around at dealers. I found new cars far out of my price range, and used models still just out of my reach. I had let go of my dream of owning this particular car when I decided to take one last look in the classified ads. There I found an ad for a privately owned, almost new model that I could afford. I made an appointment that day for a test drive and owned it within a week.

After enjoying many adventures in my Explorer for three and a half years, it became clear that I needed to raise cash to finish a project that I had been working on for some time. Selling the car looked like the best option. I was taking a risk and knew it. Would I ever own such a nice car again? Would I ever own *any* car again? Would I adjust to getting around the city on my bike and public transportation? What if I sold the car and the project failed? Then I'd have no car and no dream. I drove myself to distraction with all of the "what if's." Then one day I knew I was ready to let go of the car. I could not afford to take on extra work to raise the cash, because that would leave no time for my project. I knew I couldn't afford to let go of my *dream*—then I would truly be broke. What happened with the project? 1) you are reading it; and 2) I have become an avid cyclist.

All of us are challenged to take risks, to let go of comfort (even if we know it isn't good for us) in order to grow, to make room for more abundance. We let go of relationships, jobs, living arrangements, eating habits, hair styles, cars and all kinds of attachments. We take a leap of faith. We have to take the risk of letting go before the universe will reveal what it has in mind to replace it. *That's risky*. We want to see what's behind door number three before we give up our year's supply of Eskimo Pies.

We may be more fearful of actually *getting* what we want, than not achieving our dreams. Then we might have to be happy! What *if* we related to our work, family, significant relations, and higher power out of a full expression of joy? Can we risk that much goodness, that much *enthus*iasm in our lives? Will we recognize ourselves in this joy? Will others? Perhaps that is just what we need to do—re-*cognize* ourselves as channels of universal passion.

Some of us tried to evade the risk of disappointment by letting go of hopes, dreams, and passions altogether. If we do not allow ourselves to know what we want in the first place, then we won't feel the loss and/or shame of not getting it. We decide in advance that we don't deserve a month off to travel, or we probably couldn't cut it in graduate school anyway, and we'd most likely botch that family room redecorating job we've been dying to start, too. It becomes easier to let go of the passion than to head into such uncharted territories.

If we practice LISTEN TO YOUR ESSENCE, then we can trust our passion to be true. As we allow ourselves to feel the rush of excitement, anticipation, and curiosity, we are swept away by discovery. There is nothing to lose if we approach our passions as humble students; all we risk is the possibility of learning from our experiences. When we practice FOLLOW YOUR PASSION it appears that we choose a life of risk, but if we value our vision above an illusion of security, we have nothing to lose by pursuing it. Vision cannot be lost or taken away, unless we choose to lose it or give it away. Our reward may be new experiences, joy, passion, and, yes, finding ourselves in uncharted territories where our world defines itself according to new rules—or according to *no* rules at all. This will challenge those of us practicing **PER-FECTIONISM**.

My friend Peter decided to heed his inner rumblings and signed up for that yoga class he'd been thinking about for months. He sent in the registration fee, bought new sweat pants, and headed to the community center for his first class. The room was cozy and the instructor had lowered the lights and lit incense. Peter took a deep breath and gave himself over to the experience.

The instructor encouraged the students not to worry about doing it right. "This is not a competition," she said, "Keep your attention on your own experience and your own journey." The first exercise she demonstrated was the "Salute to the Sun." Peter followed her lead and soon became frustrated. His legs were stiff from years of sitting in front of a computer terminal. He couldn't even touch the floor with his finger tips (and he couldn't help but notice the instructor's hands were flat on the ground, as were a few of the other supposed "beginners"). By the end of the class Peter felt more tense than when he came in. He felt he had failed.

Soon after the first class he recognized that his perfectionism had cut himself off from the experience. He later told me of his life-long obsession, "If I can't do it perfectly, then I don't want to try at all. If I can't be Mother Teresa, then I don't even want to be nice to people." I encouraged him to go back, citing advice given to me when I was learning sign language: "Anything worth doing, is worth doing badly."

When we give ourselves permission to be awkward beginners, we have the opportunity to make new discoveries. "Experts" may struggle to take in new information. The beginner is an empty cup, ready to be filled. If we expect perfection from ourselves in every endeavor, we will never find the creative opportunity; we will be too focused on getting it right to recognize inspiration even if it hits us over the head. We also learned to give our creative power to **OTHER PEOPLE**.

Other people can be formidable obstacles in our pursuit of passion. Nay-sayers, energy-drainers, and envy-ers all provide excellent distractions. They prevent us from following, or even *knowing*, our passion. We are in dangerous territory when we give other people that much power. A wise woman said, "If the other person is the problem, there is no solution." As long as we blame other people for our circumstances, we have no power to change them. When the problem is out *there*, we avoid responsibility for it. We choose not to respond.

When we ask what *we* can change about our experience, we have power again. We are no longer victims. This is an incredibly liberating experience. Freedom comes, in part, by:

DOING THINGS DIFFERENTLY

Sometimes the simplest possibilities elude us. We forget to *ASK FOR HELP.*

Seek the company of people who celebrate your passion. One of the most valuable lessons in my own spiritual recovery is that I cannot do it alone and, since I've begun doing things differently, I realize—why would I want to!?!

Help comes in many forms: support groups, trusted friends, and spiritual relationships. It also comes from unexpected places; I have found just the solution I needed from enthusiastic reference librarians, my students, fellow writers, teaching colleagues, gas station attendants, my public speaking colleagues, and many others. We never know where our mentors are until we seek them. They are hard-pressed to help us if we don't ask!

For those of us battling (and often losing to) the voices of fear and judgment on a daily basis, help is available in formal and informal relationships. The A.R.T.S. (Artists Recovering Through the Steps) program recommends getting a "creative buddy" with whom to "bookend." This is a support person with whom to talk about hopes, fears, and a daily creative action plan. One buddy may call and say, "Today I'm going to call the travel agent and see if there are any cheap fares to that electric train convention in St. Louis." The next morning she calls this buddy to report whether or not she made the call. "Bookending" provides accountability, which in turn fosters responsibility to our creative process. In the early stages of our creative recovery we may not take seriously commitments we whisper to ourselves, but we might just honor those we say out loud to a trusted supporter who will want to know whether or not we followed through.

One of the first creativity workshops I led has continued to meet on its own for years. Its members share works-in-progress, lives-in-progress, and enthusiastically support each others' gallery openings, performances, and readings (many of these people would not have dared to call themselves creative a few years ago!). The group is a collective "creative buddy" that inspires passion.

At the same time we seek support for passion, we must weed out those well-meaning saboteurs who rain on our parade. There is a difference between honest, loving response of trusted friends (which gives us an opportunity determine whether or not we have been swept away by a "quick fix" passion) and veiled remarks of those ultimately threatened by our passion.

The most loving response is often to **FOLLOW YOUR FEAR**. Follow my fear!?! Yes. Fear is often an indicator that we are close to creative pay-dirt. Sometimes it is fear of a challenge that requires us to reach to new heights, fear of a discovery that may change our life direction, or fear of a breakthrough that leads to a new level of self-knowledge.

A few years ago I was invited to speak at a national conference of creativity experts. Until then, I had comfortably presented seminars to business people, educators, and nonprofit groups. These people were always thirsty for what I had to say, and rarely were there any creativity authorities present. Suddenly I was going to be reviewed by others who were experts in the field! I rose to the occasion by focusing on my message and the aspects that were unique to my work. It turned out to be a wonderful, reaffirming experience that allowed me to take my own work to a new level. What an opportunity I would have missed had I given in to fear and self-doubt!

Most of us have had similar experiences. Of course we will be afraid of the unknown, the new experiences, the big challenges. But if we choose to, we can use fear like a divining rod to home in on the mother lode of our creative process.

Fear is a big ugly monster, frothing at the mouth, wildly waiving its tentacles as it guards the door of our passion. It wants us to believe that what lurks behind that door is even worse than the "fear monster." It *does* take courage to walk through that door, because what awaits is an opportunity to step into our lives and experience ourselves in a way we never before dreamed possible. We might even discover what it is like to be happy. Then what would we have to complain about?

Fear is a subversive smoke screen that keeps us from moving forward. Underneath may lie our deepest passion. Let me repeat the definition of courage from Chapter One: fear meeting faith. Feel the fear and *FOLLOW* YOUR PASSION. Value your ideas and inspirations. Don't wait around for someone else to encourage you or drag you to that dog show, management seminar, or Israeli folk dance you want to attend. Give your passion the space and support it needs. Essence is the source of inspiration. Passion is the source of action. When your Essence inspires your curiosity and gives you joy—heed the call.

Jeff found the courage to follow his passion, despite the warnings of friends and family.

> *A few years ago I heard about and saw a company and product that made my heart start to race. I had been employed by a fortune-fifty company for thirteen years where I had a very successful career. Upon seeing this new revolutionary technology, I was drawn to it like a moth to a flame. I could not stop thinking about it and how right my background was for selling it. I told my family about it and they thought that I was crazy for even thinking about leaving my current employer. My burning desire to be involved with this new company continued and I made up my mind to get hooked-up with them. I knew it was going to be difficult to get a job with this company because of its high profile and popularity, but for some reason everything magically fell into place. It has been two years since I made this move to this company and it has been wildly successful and more rewarding than I ever could have imagined. I owe this all to following my passion and not listening to the voices of fear and judgment.*

As we begin to practice FOLLOW YOUR PASSION (and even once we are well into the journey) it is easy to become distracted by others' passions or, as I discussed earlier, by all of the "shoulds" which inundate us everyday. Do not mistake someone else's path for your own—FOLLOW **YOUR** PASSION.

Remember—the road may not always be easy. The more powerful the path, in terms of potential for personal growth and success, the more vigorously the universe challenges our commitment to it and offers us excuses to throw in the towel. But, as my fortune read after a recent Chinese meal, "Your path is difficult, but you will be amply rewarded."

Sometimes the reward will be the path itself and the exhilaration of full participation in your life. When Leonardo DiVinci was asked to name his greatest achievement, he responded, "Leonardo DiVinci." If we are always looking outside ourselves for the fruits of our labor, we may miss the true reward.

CHAPTER FOUR

Abstain From Judgment

As a young girl Susan spotted a paint set in the dime store and decided she wanted to be a painter. She saved her nickels and dimes and made a secret trip early one Saturday morning to buy the 36-color paint set, two sizes of brushes, and a pad of paper. When the rest of the family was sufficiently distracted by the business of the day, Susan slipped down to the basement with her shiny new supplies. A peg board wall served as a make-shift easel. Soon Susan was immersed in the world of painting. She spent hours in her secret artist's cove. She hurried home from school and got up early on weekends to make time for her passion, away from the relentless teasing of four sisters.

One day at her school library Susan saw an art book filled with the work of

Van Gough, O'Keefe, Duchamp, Kahlo, and other masters. She eagerly brought the book home and pored over it. As she stared into the work of those who had spent their lives developing art, her heart sank. She looked at those beautiful, detailed paintings in the book, and then to her eight-year-old child's watercolors. In a moment Susan decided that the work which had been the source of such joy and passion was a horrible waste of time—and a dismal failure. She closed the library art book and crumpled up her paintings, burying them deep in the laundry room trash can. She put away her paint set for the last time and slipped back upstairs— unnoticed.

THE PRINCIPLE

Judgment is the most insidious block to creativity. Most of us have at least one story of an experience that shut down all or part of our passion. Self-judgment, censorship, criticism, and merciless comparison damage as much as the judgment of others. Judgment destroys the wonder so necessary to appreciating life's possibilities. Without it we would still live, quite literally, in the dark ages. Discovery propels us forward. We are all born with a desire to play; it was how we learned about ourselves and our world. It is how we *continue* to learn. We forget that.

Tammy Slater, a project manager for a construction firm, discovered the profound impact of judgment on her life. "I spent the better part of my life judging myself and, therefore, my creativity, as lacking.... What allowed me to recognize the creativity I'd possessed all along was finally becoming sick and tired of seeking approval from outside of myself."

Many of us suffered early on from the judgment of others. Carole Cirignani, a sales promotion manager, remembers the exact moment she lost her joy of writing.

> *I loved to write. I would write music, poems, and letters. I even wrote love letters for a girlfriend whose beau was in the Army and I continued to enjoy writing until my college writing class in 1973. I was excited to be there and thought I would do well. Boy did I get in over my head. We had an in-class essay assignment on the second day. I handed mine in and for some reason the instructor decided to choose my essay to rip apart in front of the whole class. My heart was ripped along with my essay. I dropped the class and stopped writing all together. No more poems, lyrics for songs, or letters. This instructor had a profound effect on me. I lacked confidence in my ability to write. Her criticism meant, to me, that I was not good enough.*

Judgment has paralyzing power. Through different life experiences, both Tammy and Carole were left with the same result—lack of confidence and fear of expressing their true voice.

Though the creative process is non-linear and defies compartmentalization, it is helpful to think of it in terms of three equally important stages: Generation, Evaluation, and Implementation.

GENERATION

I liken this stage to an open faucet, where we allow our ideas to flow freely, without fear of censorship from ourselves or others. Roger von Oech, Ph.D. calls this the germinal stage[35], because it incubates and nurtures new ideas and impulses. Brainstorming, one of the oldest idea-generation techniques, supports this stage of the creative process.

EVALUATION

Here we step back and take a look at our buckets full of ideas and options. We decide which are innovative and worth exploring, cost-effective, or just plain seem like fun. We also decide which ideas need more incubation. All creative processes, even improvisation, pass through the evaluation stage. Whether it happens in a split second or over months of deliberation, it is a pivotal focusing stage of the creative process.

IMPLEMENTATION

This third, and often overlooked, stage is where the rubber hits the road—where we do the footwork to bring our passion to life. Businesses lamenting the failure of their creativity training are often disappointed when the wonderful ideas developed there do not make it into practice. This is often due to a breakdown in the Implementation Stage—characterized by confusion and lack of accountability.

These three stages have equal value. Trouble begins when we give one more value than another, rushing through the Generation Stage, in order to get on with the Evaluation Stage. Even more damaging is evaluating or *judging* our ideas while still in the Generation Stage, before the ideas are fully formed. Author Judith Guest says, "The 'creator' and the 'editor'—two halves of the writer whole—

should sleep in separate rooms."[36] We censor our impulses as stupid or impractical before we have even begun to explore their possibilities. This is abusive and destructive to our creative process; it simply is not possible to simultaneously judge and be receptive to possibilities.

Generation Stage critical judgment is like a gardener who, in her desire to grow champion tomatoes, evaluates each plant's potential just as it peeks through the soil, and chooses at that point either to destroy or nurture the seedling based on that evaluation.

We call parents who are critical of their children unreasonable, at best, and abusive, at worst. These external voices of judgment are soon internalized—played over and over again into adulthood. Tammy remembers, "Prior to confronting my father's alcoholism and our family response to it, I spent a great deal of time in self-criticism and had a very low value of myself—the essential part of me."

Dianna Krus described the effect of her self-judgment in team meetings at work:

> I would harshly judge every opinion I had before
> voicing it. If the idea survived my barrage of
> questioning, fault-finding, and measuring up to
> everyone else's comments, then I would voice the
> idea. Needless to say, I did not participate too
> much at meetings. I rarely attacked others' ideas
> with the same venom I used on myself.

We see clearly the destructive power of judgment here, yet we commit the same crimes against our *own* creative process without batting an eye. "That's a crazy idea!" "No one will respect you again if you say that!" "You're too old to try that!" Or, "You're too young to try that!" We say to ourselves what we would never dream of saying to a loved one or to someone whom we wanted to support.

Creativity in Business authors Ray and Myers call these negative messages the "VOJ" (Voice of Judgment). [37] In *Writing Down the Bones,* Natalie Goldberg calls her censor "the editor,"[38] while people recovering from the addictive process simply say "that's the disease talking." Whatever name you choose for this destructive self-talk, know that these messages are not true. They are not you.

ABSTAIN FROM JUDGMENT is rooted in the wisdom of recovery programs. An alcoholic knows that the first step toward recovery is to stop drinking, to abstain from the behavior that is causing so much pain. Only then will there be room for life to rush in. Likewise, we must stop judging for the full resources of our imagination to become available.

Quantum physicists have discovered that judgment (or, more appropriately, scientific expectation) profoundly affects the outcome of subatomic particle experiments. As I discussed in Chapter One, before being measured, particles cannot be said to have a specific momentum or location. This is not because the scientists or their equipment are inadequate; it is simply the nature of the subatomic world— it is expressed in terms of potential and probability.

In particle experiments, when information about the momentum of an electron is sought, only general information about the location can be obtained. Likewise, the more accurately the location is measured, the less accurately the momentum can be measured, according to the Heisenberg Uncertainty Principle. Observing the atom disturbs it. Therefore the outcome of the observation is affected. It is impossible for the observer *not* to participate in or influence the world he observes.

The observer's or participant's relationship to the sub-atomic world mirrors our relationship to the early stages of the creative process. Before we judge, impulses and ideas have unlimited potential. The are processes, rather than products—with each possibility as viable as the next. As soon as we place a value judgment on an idea we narrow its possibilities for expression.

Evaluation and measurement *do* have a place in the creative process, but not in the first Generation Stage. The words "evaluation," "judgment," and "criticism" are usually associated with a spectrum of value judgments. The value judgments (as in "That's a *fill-in-the-blank* idea!") grind creative energy's flow to a halt. As soon as we label our idea stupid, out-dated, horrible, or even fabulous, brilliant, innovative, we limit its potential.

Improvisation is an art form of the Generative Stage. Seasoned improvisers channel their creativity and encourage fellow players to heighten and explore discoveries on stage. These artists haven't time to censor or judge ideas. Doing so short-circuits the process. George Badecker, a New York performer and improvisation teacher, sees the impact of judgment in his students.

> *There's this issue of wanting to be funny. I see people checking themselves and instead of following their first impulse, which may be the more interesting, dramatic, or moving possibility, I see them trying to be funny rather than going with their instinct. They have a preconceived notion that improvisation has to be funny, and they censor out anything that doesn't fit that notion.*

How often have we, like novice improvisers, censored our speech or actions, because we thought we knew in advance what was expected or "right" for the situation. When we judge, we cut the creative process off at the knees. When we ABSTAIN FROM JUDGMENT we remove the obstacles to the natural and passionate flow of our creative life energy. To free ourselves of these chains, we need to fiercely confront our:

LEARNED BLOCKS

Early on I learned to believe that I could increase my value—my status—by criticizing others. Perhaps I misunderstood, but I thought the saying was: *"IF YOU CAN'T SAY SOME-THING CRITICAL, DON'T SAY ANYTHING AT ALL."* Life was a competition, and criticism was one of my most effective weapons to diminish the perceived opponents. Judgment, or assigning value to people and their ideas, gives us an *illusion* of having power over ourselves and others. The problem is just that—it is an illusion.

I honed my formidable judgment skills as an undergraduate theatre student, watching countless productions and participating in as many formal (and informal) critique sessions. We were trained in the fine art of criticism. We were taught the elements that comprised a "successful" production, and attended shows like vultures, waiting for friends and colleagues to slip up, so that we could feast on their shortcomings at post-show discussions.

These sessions were rarely for the benefit of the creators, but for us—the student observers, to prove how much we knew and to prove that, if the offending production had been in *our* hands, we certainly would have avoided the obvious mistakes our classmates had made.

My classmates and I did not learn about the Generation Stage of the creative process, or about appropriate response, or that the educational environment should, first and foremost, be a safe place to take risks. Nor were we taught the role of failure in the development of our work. Rather, we learned the adage that you are only as good as your last show. Almost every profession has an equivalent saying— "You are only as good as your last *fill-in-the-blank* (case, book, sale, presentation, project, etc.)" To our detriment, we did not learn the difference between judgment and clear response (See this chapter's "Doing Things Differently").

Sadly, I was not alone in my experience. Students and professionals in almost every domain report a top priority was to root out flaws in their colleagues. Mara, a lawyer and artist, remembers her law school training and the impact it had on her creative life:

> *Law is taught by the Socratic Method. This is about testing someone from every angle. We would stand up in class and be grilled about a case. We were always on the watch for something that we'd done wrong or said wrong. Law schools justify how they train us, because it's how they believe we will experience it outside.... Mistakes can be very dramatic in law. I can understand why we lawyers are so cautious, because the stakes are so high, and the standard is perfection. The result is that we become our own judges. This cuts us off from seeing all of the possibilities. When I stopped practicing law, it was very freeing. It has taken me a long time to get rid of my internal judge. I had to learn to set my lawyer brain aside and let go of cause and effect thinking.*

Mara, like so many others, learned that the sharp blade (or tongue) of judgment cuts both ways. We cannot use it on others without injuring ourselves in the process, because we also learned to **JUDGE YOUR OWN IDEAS FIRST, BEFORE ANYONE ELSE HAS THE CHANCE.**

This process begins innocently; we learned it was impolite to blow our own horn. That soon turned into our inability to accept compliments from others, and that, in turn, evolved into full-blown self-criticism. Many times I have found myself in a rehearsal, or other creative process, distracted by the negative reviews the committee in my head is writing, or putting words to the most viscous self-criticism.

It's a powerful distraction, self-abuse. Suzanne, a model, discovered the potentially debilitating power of this block working in a competitive environment. "When I'm working, if I think about people judging me, then I no longer feel free to express myself."

Linna, (who embraced her passion for dance later in life—Chapter Three) finds freedom from self-judgment and the judgment of others in her spirituality. "When I listen to and obey my higher power, I move forward. There is no conflict. When I mistakenly believe I need to please other people, that's when I get confused and lose my way."

At first this self-criticism seemed a useful shelter from the criticism of others. After all, if I shoot down my own ideas first, I won't have to suffer the pain of hearing the judgment I imagine will come from others.

Just as Susan decided that her early paintings didn't measure up to the masters, we too, find reason to abort our early, awkward and unformed ideas. If we find evidence to support our fear that we are not the next Madam Currie or George Washington Carver (and who couldn't find such evidence in the formative stages of any pursuit?), we put ourselves out of our misery by letting go of our passion altogether.

We may also distract ourselves by asking *"HOW AM I DOING SO FAR?"* We become entertainers furiously tap dancing with sweat pouring, limbs flying–desperately trying to please the audience. When we look up from the Generation Stage to see if we have approval from whomever we've assigned that role, we abandon the process. Our creativity becomes about listening to *someone else's* Essence rather than our own. We must delight *ourselves* before we can hope to move others.

Judgment may also rear its ugly head disguised as *GRANDIOSITY/ATROCITY*. We ride the judgment pendulum to its extremes; one extreme leads to riches and *Oprah* appearances; the other to public humiliation. When we are in this destructive cyclone, it is uncanny how much evidence we find to propel us to new heights of tortured (and, thankfully, distorted) thinking.

After seminars I sometimes ask participants to fill out evaluation sheets so that I can continue to improve. Early in my career, the temptation was to interpret each comment as wildly positive or desperately negative. An innocent "Great workshop! You are an intelligent and inspiring speaker" fostered visions of hosting my own TV program, while a "Needed more time for the exercises and discussion" had me reconsidering my life's work altogether. Had I only known about the third option–to take in the response, if it is useful, and stay on course toward my own personal vision and passion.

Both extremes of the pendulum destroy the joy of the process. Both cut us off from a full experience of what is. Ironically, Grandiosity/Atrocity also places us at the imagined center of the universe. Even self-abusive thoughts are ultimately self-centered or, as they say in recovery circles, we believe we are "the biggest piece of shit the world ever revolved around." These distorted, self-centered thoughts, however, serve only to take us *out* of our true center and away from our Essence.

We will also be thrown off center if we believe **JUDG-MENT ASSIGNS VALUE**. As we now know, there is a place for evaluating the merits of our creative impulses—*after* we give full attention to the Generation Stage. Evaluating may be editing, revising, reworking, discussing, or simply letting go of ideas about which we feel less passion. None of these processes needs to assign value judgments. Doing so can have severe impact on the creator, as well as on the creative process.

Most of us have opportunities to ABSTAIN FROM JUDGMENT, whether deciding which movie to see, generating ideas to increase company profits, or solving a family conflict. We do not always seize these opportunities due to years of practicing judgment. Here are more ideas to break free by:

DOING THINGS DIFFERENTLY

The mechanistic model thrives on dualism—either we judge emerging ideas, or we don't say anything at all and are at the mercy of ideas and impulses with all levels of merit. A third option is to **DISTINGUISH BETWEEN JUDGMENT AND RESPONSE**. Response provides useful information to the recipient, without judging the idea or its source.

Again, we take a lesson from the physicists who discovered that the very act of observation influenced what they observed. Today we acknowledge that there is rarely such a thing as a truly objective observer. Subatomic physicists, social scientists, and documentary filmmakers unavoidably impact their subjects. In the arts, the viewer is often thought of as an observer, as well as a participant in the creation of the collective experience.

Whereas judgment-laden response focuses on the object as separate from the observer, clear response focuses on the experience of the observer as participant and does not assume that the observer/participant's perception is the only one possible.

An observer/participant-centered response to a playwright after the first reading of his new play might be, "I felt confused when the drifter character launched into a monologue about his mother in the second act." Here, the creator is not judged or shut down, but is given potentially useful information as she develops her work.

A less effective response is what I call "product-centered response." Rather than focus on the observer's experience, it fixates on the idea, product, or worse, on the idea-originator. The product-centered response to our hypothetical theatrical work-in-progress might go something like: "That second act monologue doesn't work You should cut it and lose that pointless drifter, too." The message is similar in both versions, however the observer/participant-centered response offers opportunity and opens doors, while the product-centered response constricts every creative impulse in its path, limiting possibilities.

When we speak in terms of our own experience, we keep the focus on ourselves without threatening the collaborative process or passing judgment. It is all too easy to state opinions or fears as facts, or to believe that others' responses are facts. Feedback is as essential to the evolution of any creative process, as it is to natural systems traveling through seemingly chaotic stages. However, if the response, or the responder, is given too much power we can be thrown off center and lose touch with our own instincts and Essence. We all see our experiences in the context of our personal world view. This makes for a wonderful diversity of perspectives. It is confusing when we forget there may be more than one response to our evolving work.

For this reason, we also need to **ASK FOR APPROPRIATE RESPONSE**. Even the clearest, most well-intentioned response distracts, at best or, destroys, at worst, if received prematurely. In the development stages of a show, I invite a few trusted observers to witness the evolving work. During the early Generation Stage of development, I do not want detailed responses about the outward manifestation of the piece. I *do* want general responses about the spirit and general shape of the story, and the textures of the piece. I save the details for the Evaluation Stage, when we edit, shape, and polish.

It took me several uncomfortable experiences to learn to ask for the appropriate response for the Generation Stage in the process, as well as to **REFUSE TO JUDGE EMERGING IDEAS**. Again, this does not mean that, at the appropriate time, we don't step back and evaluate our ideas and decide which ones we want to put energy into. We *do* continue to abstain from assigning value judgments of good or bad.

Try turning all response into positive feedback. Ideas To Go, Inc. in Minneapolis developed a concept they call "Forness." Focus on what you are "for" about an idea or inspiration and turn negative reactions into constructive feedback. For example, instead of saying, "I don't see how we can take this project any further; it clearly is too expensive," we search for the positive spin; "I'd like to see how we can make this plan more cost-effective, so that it will fit into next year's budget." "For-ness" is a wonderful way to give clear response without judging either the idea or the originator of the idea.

RESPOND TO YOUR VOICE OF JUDGMENT. Keep track of your internal litany of judgments designed to keep creative energy in check. Write them down. Then write a rebuttal. Or perform a ritual burning of your judgments and blocks (over the sink, please). Try practicing the same technique that motivational speaker and author, Wayne Dyer, uses when negative thoughts enter his mind—cut them off by saying, "Next!"

Or try the technique that has been passed on by creative writing instructors everywhere. Legend has it that John Steinbeck kept a pad of paper next to his typewriter when he was writing *Of Mice and Men*. On it went all of his self-doubts and criticism: "This is horrible!" "Who ever told you that you could write?" "My editor will have a good laugh reading *this* chapter!" Listing these internal grumblings temporarily silenced them so he could continue his work until the next judgmental outburst. He patiently gave the committee in his head their "air time," and then proceeded to write one of the classics of American literature.

It matters not whether our inspirations come in ideas, images, words, or an eight-year-old's watercolors; they each deserve the time and care to emerge. By practicing ABSTAIN FROM JUDGMENT we create the space for our creativity to live, breathe, and flourish.

CHAPTER FIVE

Say, "Yes, and..."

George remembers one of his experiences as a beginning improv student at the Players Workshop in Chicago. "I was in a scene with this woman where we were having a picnic by a campfire. The scene was going along nicely, when all of a sudden the woman got up and said, 'Hey, look at this boat!' and she got in the boat and motioned for me to join her. Well, I had decided that there were many more possibilities with the picnic and the camp fire, so I was trying to get her to come back to the picnic. I didn't want to let go of the picnic. We struggled with this for a while when our instructor yelled from offstage, JUST GET IN THE BOAT!' I had in my mind where the scene was supposed to go and I was resisting this new discovery. Once I got in the boat, the scene started moving again. That was a very important lesson."

THE PRINCIPLE

The first principle improvisation students learn, SAY, "YES, AND...," is central to the success of this art form. When improvisers say "no" to what is offered in the moment, the creative/collaborative process stops dead in its tracks.

Experienced improvisers know that they must practice SAY, "YES, AND...," not only to move the scene forward, but to gain the trust of their fellow players. In their book *Truth in Comedy,* Del Close, Charna Halpern, and Kim "Howard" Johnson say:

> *...this is a very relaxing way in which to work. A player knows that anything he says on stage will be immediately accepted by his fellow player, and treated as if it were the most scintillating idea ever offered to mankind. His partner then adds on to his idea, and moment by moment, the two of them have created a scene that neither of them had planned.*[39]

When I take my beginning improv students to their first fully improvised show, they are in awe. The characters and stories seem to evolve so effortlessly, and at times the comedy is so hilarious, the drama so poignant, that it is hard to believe there was no scripting or rehearsing. The awe wears off back in the classroom as my novice improvisers learn that good improvisation is not about thinking of brilliant lines or assuming peculiar voices. Nor is it about trying to be funny, dramatic, or touching. It is simply about getting out of the way of their own creative energy, to SAY, "YES, AND..." to the discoveries and ideas of their fellow players. They discover that the brilliant moments they enjoyed came from accepting whatever is given and adding to it (not necessarily the result of comic genius).

It is just as important to say *"and"* as it is to say "yes." In improvisation circles, we describe each discovery we make and offering we receive from our fellow players as a gift. Our job is to open that gift, marvel at its beauty, and then give something back of equal or greater value.

Some years ago, I was asked to direct a murder mystery dinner theatre show. Though more conservative and commercial than most of my work, I agreed. It was a nice break from the long development processes of original theatre, and (let's face it) I needed the money. During the rehearsal process, my friend, Peter Siragusa (who regularly stopped by rehearsals), and I had the somewhat ambitious thought that we could write something better than this and went to work on a script. Peter performed at night, and I worked days, which left little time to write together. We solved the problem by meeting at a diner near my office to practice SAY, "YES, AND..." over our sandwiches and fries.

We each brought a note pad and wrote and talked as fast as we could (I have the ketchup-stained notes to prove it!). We roughed out the entire play and improvised the dialogue by building on each other's ideas. Sometimes the seed idea was less than stellar, but when we added to it, it became something funny, unusual, or surprising. On weekends, we typed and edited our notes. The dinner theatre producer loved the script and decided to produce the show. In rehearsals we continued to SAY, "YES, AND..." with the director and cast. While the final script will not be recorded as one of the cornerstones of American theatre, it was one of my most refreshing collaborative experiences because it was developed in the spirit of SAY, "YES, AND...," and it even enjoyed a year-and-a-half run in downtown Chicago!

Conscious of it or not, we improvise from the moment we wake up to the moment we drift off to sleep each day. In large and small ways our lives offer "gifts" at each turn: an unexpected loss, a new co-worker from a culture other than our own, a bounced check, a new romantic attraction, a sale on nectarines, a canceled lunch date.... In the spirit of SAY, "YES, AND..." each of these are opportunities. They are nagging inconveniences or the source of great suffering if we choose to fight against them and say "no!" to the gifts dotting our path.

It is not possible to avoid pain; however, it is possible to avoid suffering. We suffer when we try to wrestle life to the ground and make it behave on *our* terms. We can live fulfilling, creative lives when we accept what we are given and build on it.

Art Blake, a former student, unwittingly provided a wonderful opportunity for his children to practice SAY, "YES, AND..."

> *Both of my children have a chore to do each day; but on Saturdays they have a few more than normal. As with most kids, they don't like doing chores. I tried something different with them last Saturday and got a nice surprise. When I asked them to do their chores I gave them the choice to do which chores they wanted. They could also complete them their own way. When I returned, I was surprised that they were finished with their chores in less than an hour, because they helped each other to complete the chores. They now do their chores together, because they realize how much quicker they can finish. It dawned on me that I was telling them how I wanted the chores done, and it took them longer and they didn't enjoy it at all. Now they don't mind them at all, plus, they have found out they work well together.*

SAY, "YES, AND..." is a principle of collaboration. Art gave his children an opportunity to SAY, "YES, AND..." by giving them choices. They then found it was in their best interest to work together, to SAY, "YES, AND..." to each other, in order to attain their shared goal (finishing their chores as soon as possible). A workshop participant recently likened it to an electric circuit. "When we SAY, "YES, AND..." the circuit is unbroken; all the lights remain on, and no one is left out. No one's contribution is denied or belittled."

Scientists have discovered that at very low temperatures certain materials have the ability to conduct the flow of electricity with minimal resistance. These materials are called superconductors. The most common conductor of household electricity, copper wire, gets warm due to the resistance that occurs when electrons collide with each other and with copper atoms, resulting in wasted energy. In a superconductor at low temperature electrons are less likely to collide and the electrons loose less energy to heat, making for a highly efficient system for conducting energy.[40]

Just as superconducting materials readily conduct electrical energy, we become superconductors of our individual and organizational creative energy when we SAY, "YES, AND...." We recover our creative spirit as we let go of the obstacles of judgment, control, perfectionism, and many other roadblocks which slow and distort the flow of creative energy. By practicing SAY, "YES, AND..." we become a conduit for the flow of what is essentially and completely us.

Our collaborative relationships and organizations can be superconductors of collective creative energy, as well. When we apply SAY, "YES, AND..." and ABSTAIN FROM JUDGMENT, we remove two key obstacles to the free flow of creativity. Several levels of collaboration are possible: collaboration with Essence, collaboration with environment, collaboration with another person, and group collaboration. Each provides opportunities to practice SAY, "YES, AND...."

When we work alone, it is easy to forget that we are in a collaborative relationship. "It's all me," we think; "I have to rely solely on my own resources!" In fact, when we practice LISTEN TO YOUR ESSENCE, we are participating in the most important collaborative relationship of all—a relationship with the source of our creativity. When we listen to this source and accept what we hear and build on it, our work evolves and we don't get stuck. When we think we're doing it alone, the well sometimes runs dry and we feel as if we have exhausted our resources.

When we pay attention we also collaborate with our environment. A news story, poem, TV repair person, cereal box label, or telemarketing call are all potential "gifts" to keep our creative energy flowing.

One-on-one collaborations are other easily over looked opportunities. Deidre Brightman, a property manager says:

> The principle, SAY, "YES, AND..." helps me a mini-
> mum of three to five times a day. And that's on a
> slow day! In negotiating with existing tenants or
> listening to their complaints or problems, it's
> important not to cut them off or say, 'That's not
> going to work' or 'That's not the way we've done
> it.' When I throw in the words "Yes, and..." some-
> where in the first sentence, I can feel the person
> on the other end of the telephone opening up.

Whether on a team project at work, planning a vacation with friends, or creating a community mural, we can practice SAY, "YES, AND..." to tap into the collective resources of the group. Nachmanovitch says, "...inertia, which is often a major block in solitary work, hardly exists at all here: A releases B's energy; B releases A's energy. Information flows and multiplies easily. Learning becomes many-sided, a refreshing and vitalizing force."[41]

When we approach life looking for opportunities to collaborate, to SAY, "YES, AND..." we find that the world opens up rather than resists. This is true whether we collaborate with our Essence, the world around us, unexpected life circumstances, individuals, or groups. When we accept and add to the gifts, our creative energy grows and transforms—often into something quite surprising, something that we would never have imagined had we not been willing to participate in life as a collaborative opportunity.

SAY, "YES, AND..." takes advantage of the abundant diversity of our fellow human beings, whether in the work place or elsewhere in our lives. Instead of viewing our differences as obstacles, we can acknowledge and accept them (say, "Yes!" to them) and build on the ideas, perspectives and energy they provide.

Robert Hayles, Ph.D., 1996 President of the American Society of Training and Development, and an international diversity consultant and trainer says, "'Yes, and...' is something I routinely try to practice when I'm doing diversity training. The use of 'and' is a powerful facilitation tool."[42] Tension arises when we attempt to control the diversity inherent to the creative process; invest in a specific outcome and all possibilities contrary to it appear as threats.

Physicists are working on a unified field theory to explain gravity, radiation, and the forces in the atom as manifestations of the same force. The wave-particle duality and the inescapable uncertainty of measuring electron location and momentum are only a few such paradoxical phenomena already mentioned. Nature is a master of SAY, "YES, AND...."

For us humans, accepting differences and contradictions challenges our comfort zone. The scientific model, as we have seen, is based in the mechanistic view of the world. When scientists discovered that the world does not always act as a machine, they found it quite unsettling. Einstein and other early contributors to quantum theory, challenged the belief that the subatomic world was not deterministic and orderly. Einstein declared, "God does not play dice."

The mysterious nature of nature could not be more godlike. The more flexible we become in accepting all possibilities as fuel for the creative fire, the more we celebrate a spirit-filled, enthusiastic life. Before we can join in the revelry, we may need to identify still more:

LEARNED BLOCKS

Wouldn't it be simpler if there really was **ONLY ONE RIGHT ANSWER?** Roger von Oech, in *A Whack on the Side of the Head*, puts the "one right answer syndrome" on his list of top ten blocks to creativity.[43] We look for one right answer and then stop when we've found *an* answer. There the discovery process stops. We settle in. That's good enough. Lost are all other possibilities.

Many of us are comfortable with clear-cut answers. It's either *this* or *that*. It cannot be both. We were taught to perceive the world this way from a very early age. School taught us that there was one right answer to every question or problem. Our job was to study hard enough (to memorize well enough) to get that one right answer. Our dualistic paradigm was born.

We experience the pain of this paradigm in our personal relationships. How many times have we pursued a point to the bitter end, only for the sake of proving ourselves *right?* How much pain have we inflicted on ourselves and others for this cause? Years ago a friend shared some words of wisdom with me as I desperately tried to get another friend to admit she had a drinking problem. I was making myself and my drinking friend miserable. She said, "Do you want to be right or do you want to be happy?" This is precisely the wisdom underlying the principle of SAY, "YES, AND...."

When we accept all possibilities—even the possibility that there may be more than one right answer, we get out of the way of creativity. We respect and support the creative processes of our collaborators, whether family members, friends, or colleagues, and allow the creative energy to flow. Not only does this wonderful force *flow* when we practice this principle, it gathers momentum, as each new possibility is added to the last.

Unless we say **"YEAHBUT...."** A staple in most Westerners' vocabulary, I have yet to find this word in any dictionary. It is a polite way to deny our own or another person's ideas, impulses, and reality. The impact is not so polite. "Yeahbut..." cuts the creative process off at the knees, because it is a form of judgment.

Unlike SAY, "YES, AND...," "Yeahbut..." does not inspire creativity or collaboration. The "Yeah" in "Yeahbut..." is not the same as the "Yes" in SAY, "YES, AND...." Rather than an unconditional acceptance and acknowledgment of the gift, the "Yeah" in "Yeahbut..." is closer to "Yeah, yeah, I know all that, but listen to *my* idea" or "Yeah, that may sound good, but let me point out the flaws before we take it any further."

Recently one of my students who works in the promotions department for a major soft drink corporation attended a brainstorming meeting for a big event co-sponsored by her company. Her immediate supervisor insisted on attending, along with representatives from several other organizations and businesses. "The purpose of the meeting was to get as many ideas out on the table as possible," said Joanne, "but my boss immediately began to criticize and evaluate each one as it was presented. It changed the entire atmosphere of the meeting. We were all very frustrated."

Perhaps Joanne's boss was suffering from a case of **EXPERT MIND**. Knowing too much (or thinking we know everything) can be a formidable block to our creativity. When advertising agencies generate new ideas for product promotions, they regularly bring in staff members from other departments who have little or no knowledge of the product or its advertising history. When the cup of knowledge is full, there is no more room for discoveries, new perspectives, or surprises.

Those who perceive themselves as experts are blocked by the knowledge of what has already been done and by what is considered acceptable practice. Barry Diller, the former Chairman of Paramount, Fox, QVC Inc., and current CEO of Silver King Communications, has learned much about "Expert Mind" in the trenches of his industry.

> *What all my experiences have had in common is a battle, a holy war if you will, between process and expertise. Expertise is a pack mentality that concludes something can't be done, or that it must be done this way. It's a mentality that relies too heavily on conventional wisdom. It has to. Because the awkward alternative would be to accept that a new thing can't be fully known or comfortably understood. Conventional wisdom, by definition, favors that which has come before, that which is known. That's great if you're build-*

ing a house or flying a plane. But it's useless, and
much worse, dangerously misleading, in creative
positions.[44]

New people in any organization are often perceived as a threat to the status quo or conventional wisdom. And they often *do* cause a disruption—enthusiastically questioning the reasons behind procedures, suggesting ways to do things more efficiently or economically. For an organization that is grounded in vision and the spirit of continuous improvement, these fresh troops are invaluable and can, when encouraged, help others see the familiar in a new way.

Unfortunately, many struggle to release their death grip on the status quo, rather than go through the unsettling process of change that can come with "doing things differently." One way we learned to maintain that illusion of control was to **OBJECTIFY IDEAS**.

Fear of losing control of, or credit for, an idea can cause us to put early limits on what it can become. In the process of trying to establish ownership, the idea or inspiration can become a thing rather than an evolving process. Certain professions may be more susceptible to this block than others; scientists, academics, and artists are only a few whose careers can be built or destroyed based on whether or not they receive proper credit for their work.

While it is certainly proper to acknowledge the source of inspiration, if we are overly vigilant in this direction we will isolate ourselves from the infinite reservoir of the collaborative process. After a certain point in collaboration, it is folly to try to keep track of what idea came from whose lips, brush, or pen. This is so not only because of the unmanageability of documenting the rush of collaborative inspiration, but because once the collective process has begun, ownership of its fruits truly belongs to the group itself. Person B may have had the idea, but it was inspired by an image from Person A, who was inspired by a phrase from Person C, who was thinking about something his fifth grade teacher said.... Without the chaotic ping-pong of ideas from collaborator to collaborator, it is unlikely that any one person would have been blessed with their inspiration.

The objectification of ideas may also have roots in the now familiar learned blocks **JUDGMENT**, **CONTROL**, and **FEAR**.

Here are three learned responses that served us well in keeping a lid on our creative life energy. It is difficult to say "Yes!" with conviction if we are in the midst of judging our own or another's idea. International corporate trainer Sivasailam Thiagarajan, Ph.D., ("Thiagi" for us linguistically-impaired Westerners) believes, "If we are worried about whether or not our ideas will work—we won't have any."[45]

George discovered this when he tried to convince his fellow improviser to rejoin him at the picnic rather than go for a boat ride. He did not initially see the possibilities of the boat ride, but later reflected:

> We could have sailed to the other side of the lake, met
> up with pirates, encountered a hurricane, or sailed
> through a fog and found ourselves in another place
> and time, but all I could see was how well the picnic
> was going and thought, 'why mess with success?'

A friend of mine recently had the revelation that all of her character defects, as she calls them, are ultimately rooted in fear.

> When I am judging others, or trying to control my
> husband to pick up his clothes, or gossiping about
> someone, I am really just acting out of my fear. I'm
> afraid to let go of control, afraid that things won't be
> okay if I let my guard down or just let people be who

*they are supposed to be—and that includes letting
ME be who I'm supposed to be!*

The good news is that we do not need to stay stuck in
the darkened room of our learned blocks, we can flip on the
light by:

DOING THINGS DIFFERENTLY

"But" is an overused word that should be trotted out only
for special occasions.

PRACTICE "BUT" ECONOMICS. Try replacing the word
"but" with the word "and," and see what a difference it
makes.

I try to practice this when I give students feedback on
their papers. Notice the difference in these two comments:

1) Frank, you've got lots of good ideas here, *but* you need to
support them with stronger evidence.

2) Frank, you've got lots of good ideas here, *and* I'd like to
see you support them with stronger evidence. *(Notice, in the
second response I also used the "for-ness" approach, saying "I'd
like to see you..." rather than "You need...")*

The first statement negates or minimizes what the student has done well by asking him to fix the paper. The second statement accepts and acknowledges the good work
and asks the student to keep building.

There are more applications of this principle. I encourage collaborators to SAY, "YES, AND..." out loud in brainstorming sessions before they throw their ideas into the

hopper. This gives each individual a chance to acknowledge what has gone before and add to it.

Brainstorming is one of the oldest tools to support collaborative creativity. The guidelines are simple: any idea goes, one person acts as the scribe, and no one is allowed to judge the ideas, no matter how crazy they sound. Seems simple enough, however I have seen many brainstorming sessions begin to breakdown only moments after they've begun. It usually starts with a snicker in response to a crazy idea or a light-hearted jibe at a co-worker. Soon people are commenting on each new idea: "We tried that last year and it was a bust;" "There's no money in the budget for something like that," "The boss will never go for it." Bam! The judgment boom has been lowered. The censor has been invited into the room. Non-verbal responses can have the same effect as vocal censorship—a frown, a roll of the eyes, a knowing glance across the table to another person. The newcomer (the most valuable player in the collaboration) or the lower status employee immediately begins to second guess her ideas. "I haven't been here long enough to say anything," "This might sound stupid. I can't risk my credibility."

Replace "but" with "and," to keep all possibilities alive. And while you're at it, practice **_BEGINNER'S MIND_**.

This is the Zen counterpart to "Expert Mind." When we approach life with beginner's mind we hold an empty cup. There is room for infinite discovery and surprise.

Many times I explore a new passion only to learn how much I don't know. This is a common experience among seekers and learners in every discipline. Rather than be overwhelmed by it, we should embrace it as innocence—a good sign that there is still room in the cup.

Even so, we can be drawn into the glass booth of "Expert Mind" where no new discoveries can reach us. How do we restore ourselves to "beginner's mind" when we have been steeped in an experience or practice for years? One way is to start again from the beginning.

Recently, I had lunch with a fellow teacher of improvisation. We both found ourselves longing for an opportunity to be beginner's again; have a safe place to fail, and to participate without the scrutiny of thirsty students looking for a demonstration of the "right way" to improvise. As we talked, it occurred to us that we could give that experience to ourselves! We formed a small group of improv teachers and peers and began to meet regularly with no goal other than to enjoy the process and rediscover what we loved so well in the art of improvisation. Each time we meet I bring my empty cup. It gives me a wonderful opportunity to reclaim beginner's mind, and to *PLAY*.

Play is an attitude. When we adopt it, stakes don't seem so high, and fear of looking foolish drops away. After all, isn't play *about* being foolish? It is much easier to SAY, "YES, AND.." when we have not given life or death, profit or loss, success or failure stakes to the game. If we approach life as Zen practitioners do—as "all practice," we release worries about doing things perfectly or whether or not it is better to stay at the picnic or go for a boat ride. Our only concern is to find the deepest enjoyment in the moment.

CHAPTER SIX

Trust the Process

After months of successful workshops for Rituals, *my collaborators and I are ready to start rehearsals, rent a theatre, and set the opening date. One week into rehearsals obstacles begin to arise. My co-writer feels a life-or-death need to leave immediately for a road trip of unspecified length; the large sanctuary space we rented is not wired for a theatre light board (a fact we discover after our borrowed light board dies a fiery death); we do not raise enough money to cover production expenses; many of the central special effects fail to work; the black and white film climax of the show regularly jams in the projector; the highly recommended mask-maker for the pivotal sun goddess character concocts a monstrosity that looks distressingly like an oversized, bright orange paper maché football hel-*

met; not to mention that in rehearsals the show itself loses the magic we all felt during those playful workshops.

As the director and producer I have many options available to me: cancel the production entirely; postpone the opening; open it as a work-in-progress, or forge ahead with the full production as originally planned. I choose to do what any seasoned director would—ignore the signs of doom and forge ahead. The looming opening date, the invited press, and all of the time and money invested create in my mind an urgency—a point of no return. Rather than disappoint the few hundred friends, family members, and adventurous theatre-goers who support us, we open the spirited, but unformed production.

While directors learn to take both positive and negative notices with a grain of salt, I feel that the headline to our "Chicago Tribune" review is perhaps too kind when it blares: "A Few Funny Bits Fail to Save Awful Rituals." *Ouch.*

THE PRINCIPLE

In the theatre our mistakes are rarely private affairs to be quietly swept under the rug. When I gathered the courage to come out of hiding after the show's opening, I realized that I learned a valuable lesson. I became so attached to the *product* of the creative process, that I abandoned the *process*.

This is one of the most difficult hurdles for beginning improvisation students (and young directors) to overcome—obsession with the product. When we worry about how we look or if we're being funny and original, we catapult ourselves out of the moment. When we focus on the product or the *result* of our creative process, we no longer fully participate in the process. This has a profoundly negative impact on the product. We become so invested in a particular outcome that we cut ourselves off from any new possibilities the creative process might present.

We have to relearn this lesson again and again. We promise ourselves we will take time to relax and enjoy life once that big project at work is completed, the kids are in school, we finish our degree, the divorce is finalized—all of the time forgetting that the process *is* the product.

Cherry Jones, winner of the 1995 Tony award for 'Best Actress in a Play,' depends on the power of the process. When asked in an interview how it felt to be called an "overnight success" more than fifteen years into her professional career, she replied:

> *This reminds me of a story my mother told me.*
> *She was taken by her mother—my grandmother—*
> *to a revival meeting in middle Tennessee in the*
> *early '30s where she was asked, "Little girl, don't*
> *you want to be saved?" And she said, "I never*
> *knew I was lost." I feel that way about "making*
> *it." I feel that every production I've gotten to work*
> *on in the last 15 years has been the greatest*
> *experience in the world. I guess in some people's*
> *eyes [I] have now made it, but that's not how I*
> *look at it."*[46]

It takes courage to release the death grip on the results of our labor. It also takes patience, according to Barry Diller:

> *Process...is ignoring the doomsayers and opti-*
> *mists alike. None of them matters. Process is fun-*
> *damentally a human function. It can't be dupli-*
> *cated or automated. It's about finding a grain of*
> *an idea and following that through to its conclu-*
> *sion. And process can't be forced or rushed. It*
> *works for everyone, not just the four or five real*
> *geniuses out there.*[47]

A former student discovered a very practical reason to practice TRUST THE PROCESS at work:

> *At my new job my objective is to acquire almost*
> *one million dollars in cost savings for our com-*
> *pany. After meeting with my customers—one*
> *being our maintenance department* —I thought it*
> *was going to be impossible. My new peers are*
> *very aggressive and abrupt, but this is not my*
> *style. By making friends with my maintenance*
> *customers and really listening to them, I've*
> *earned their trust, and together we are able to*
> *get some of these savings. I cannot just tell a*
> *department that they have to do things our way;*
> *but, by being patient, they are seeing it them-*
> *selves. By focusing on the relationships rather*
> *than the product, the product is happening natu-*
> *rally, easily, and most important (to me) jointly.*

Eastern philosophies hold this principle of valuing process and letting go of results at their core. In the Bhagavad Gita (one of the Hindu religion's central texts), Lord Krishna counsels the warrior Arjuna, "Pitiful are those who live for the fruits (of action)."[48] If we act only out of our attachment to the product of our creative energy, we will never fully express that energy or realize its possibilities; we

---

* TQM programs hold that everyone is a customer; some are internal customers, some external.

will be distracted by the transitory and illusory, rather than guided by our Essence.

Attachment limits possibility. Neurophysiologist and cognitive scientist, Francisco Varela, calls attachment to our own ideas and perceptions an "addiction to the self."[49] Just as an obsessive attachment to a substance or process can shut down the natural flow of life energy so, too, will an attachment to one specific vision or thought shut down the flow of creative energy.

A hand-lettered quotation hangs in the center of my bulletin board, above the computer in my office. A friend of mine sent it to me when I was between projects and in one of my earlier mentioned "sensory deprivation periods."

> *There is no meaning with time, no year matters,*
> *and ten years are nothing. Being an artist means,*
> *not reckoning and counting, but ripening like the*
> *tree which does not force its sap and stands con-*
> *fident in the storms of spring without fear that*
> *after them may come no summer. It does come.* [50]
>
> —RAINER MARIE RILKE

Rilke describes the process of the universe, as well as the creative process. He speaks to the universal creative spirit, when he instructs the young poet to be patient, to trust the moment. Life will flow again, ideas will come again, the storms will pass and clear the way for summer. "It does come."

Emotions often lead us through very important life processes. Grief, joy, and anger are only a few roads we might travel. Anyone who has experienced a deep loss knows that the only way to the other side is *through* it. There is no jumping ahead or sidestepping deep emotions if we truly live a creative life. Even in the darkest sadness or greatest heights of joy, the moment is all there is.

And the creative process is a living process, so like all living processes it is unpredictable, non-linear, and holistic. We cannot force, control, or contain it, though many have tried. In the middle of writing this very chapter, my ideas and words stopped flowing. I needed to move on to another part of the book and come back to this later. This chapter needed to "cook" a bit longer and, if I forced it, I would lose the integrity of the writing, rendering it hollow. When I (and it) was ready, the rest of the chapter flowed and I sailed through the sections that once stalled me. (I *did* learn something from my experience with *Rituals!).*

When we TRUST THE PROCESS life does not have to be a struggle; it is filled with the mystery and wonder we experienced as children. This is not so easy as the deceptively simple principle might suggest. Simple is not always easy. Most of us spent years doubting, blocking, or otherwise shutting down our intuitive, passionate creative process with more

LEARNED BLOCKS

I once thought a dose of **PRESCRIPTION CREATION** would heal my aching creative process. The ill-fated production of *Rituals* taught me that what worked in the past will not necessarily work in the present. I approached the show as I had the two successful original productions I had developed previously. The circumstances were similar, so why not use the same method that brought such rewards before? I mistakenly thought I had found the prescriptive formula for creating original theatre.

Too late, I discovered that the creative process is not a rash to be cured or a puzzle to be solved. Just as siblings from the same family may need very different kinds of support to thrive, so will each creative opportunity and challenge.

Whether we parent, teach, negotiate a business deal, or make art, we must approach each new child, student, business opportunity, or canvas with innocence. Experience need not destroy innocence. Our successes and challenges of the past *can* guide us, giving us confidence that, even when the path takes unexpected turns and presents obstacles, it does lead somewhere; we will reach our destination if we keep our eyes open and enjoy the journey itself.

One of the difficulties in staying in the process lies in another learned block **THE END JUSTIFIES THE MEANS**. Though Machiavelli never actually wrote these words, they reflect the essence of his 16th century philosophy of gaining and maintaining power. The product is everything. It doesn't matter how we get there, as long as we get there. As I stated earlier, this block cuts us off from important discoveries we might make along the way, not to mention from all the fun we might have. When we focus on the product to the exclusion of the process, we abandon the process *and* ourselves.

The obsessive focus on the product is really no different than an addict's obsession with the "fix." We delude ourselves that whatever it takes to get there is worth it, as long as we get there. We raise the stakes, telling ourselves that the product is so important, that we are justified in risking our health, relationships, and even our morality. And the body count can be high. Our ethics may slip, beginning with innocent white lies, then escalating to full-blown dishonesty. Our intimate relationships may suffer; professional integrity erodes; and our personality may change—all in the service of the coveted "goal."

Michele experienced this progression as an art director for an advertising agency:

> *When I had those tremendous deadlines I basically did whatever it took to get the job done. I would work without eating. I would work 80 hours a week, or more. I've worked 24 hours a day, literally without stopping. This was not uncommon. I experienced myself as completely detached from my creativity at those points and basically just did whatever it took to get the job done.*

Isn't that part of the bargain, you ask? Success stories are filled with sacrifice and tenacious one-pointed focus on achieving a vision. Yes, and those who are truly successful are open to discoveries they make on the path that may lead them in new directions. Had Scottish biologist, Alexander Fleming, exclusively focused on one result in his study of bacteria, he would have thrown out the contaminated petri dish he discovered in his lab. Instead he examined the strange mold and noticed that it had stopped the growth of the dish's original bacteria. Focusing on the process, not the product lead to the discovery of penicillin!

It is not easy to honor "mistakes" and TRUST THE PROCESS when we feel we should **BE IN CONTROL AT ALL TIMES**.

Here it is again, our friend control. We learned we should be in control of ourselves, our emotions, our career, our relationships, and ideally other people and processes. Not to be in control proved failure. Anything less than our original vision of success is a mistake. Lack of passion and motivation for our work means we are lazy. Expressed anger makes us bitches or bastards. Unless we cry; then we are wimps. If our careers take unexpected turns, we are losers...and on and on.

None of these false beliefs leaves room for other influential forces or for the fact that, no matter how much effort and good intention we put into our work, relationships, and vision, they still unfold in their own time and in their own way.

When we give in to the compulsion to control, we may mask a deeper affliction: **COWARDICE.** I originally named this block "fear." It sounded so much more noble than "cowardice." Cowardice connotes weakness of character; who wants *that* title!?! So, in an uncharacteristic attempt at manipulation, I name this block "cowardice" hoping to reach the 10-year-old child in all of us who, in response to such name-calling, puffs out his chest and says, "Who are you calling a coward!?! I'm not afraid! Just watch me!" Perhaps this will provide an opportunity to look at your fears in a new way and discover which ones are truly useful for your well-being and which hold you back.

When I ask workshop participants to name creative blocks, fear is usually at the top of the list. "Fear of failure," "Fear of looking stupid," even "Fear of success." All are ultimately rooted in a fear of losing control—fear of letting go. The irony here is that when we stop and look at the reality of our experience, try as we might, we *can't* control other people, places, things, or processes. We can't even control our own creative process. So to you long-suffering "control freaks," I say, "Let go, you coward! And try:"

DOING THINGS DIFFERENTLY

Sit down, relax, and **ASK FOR THE CUP OF TEA**. Bruce Jordan, the director and producer of the long-running murder mystery *Shear Madness*, often used a story of legendary actors Alfred Lunt and Lynn Fontaine to remind his actors to keep their performances fresh night after night, month after month. The actors, noted for their perfectionism, were nearing the end of a successful run of a show. Alfred Lunt was frustrated. "I can't understand it!," he blurted out. "I always used to get a laugh in that scene when I asked for a cup of tea. What's wrong?" "Well," mused Fontaine, "Perhaps you should go back to asking for the tea instead of for a laugh."

When we embrace the process, the product takes care of itself. This does not mean that we lack vision, but that the vision serves as a guiding force rather than a straight-jacket. Focusing on the product often destroys the lively vision that we sought in the first place.

For yet another reminder to let go, envision the Wicked Witch of the West writing this message across the sky to you: **SURRENDER, DOROTHY!!!** Sometimes we need our wake-up calls in big bold letters. Even then, we may be hit with a sudden attack of blindness or convince ourselves that this particular message was really intended for someone else *or*, if it is for us, surely it is intended for another, less chaotic time than this! Certainly there will come a time when we can spend hours in meditation and take long walks in the woods. Surely such messages are meant for times like that—not now, when we have children to raise, deadlines to meet, social obligations to attend, groceries to buy, laundry to do, and then there was that fundraising drive to organize! Surely, *not now*.

Of course, when life is at its highest pitch we *have* to surrender. We hit bottom, realizing that trying to control all of the converging processes makes everything worse, not better. In response, we throw up our hands, "That's it. I give up! I just can't do any more!" And occasionally, we have the presence of mind and spirit to surrender well before we lose ourselves in the sometimes raging rivers of life.

I have many opportunities to "Surrender, Pamela!" these days. In the past few years I spoke to organizations or designed a seminar for a company once every few months. This provided a nice balance to my teaching, writing, and directing. I planned weeks, sometimes months, in advance—researching, outlining, preparing handouts and slides, then rehearsing and rehearsing and rehearsing. As my presentation day drew near, I focused my energy. I let friends and family know I could not see them until after the event was over. Upon its completion, I let out a big sigh of relief, gave myself a few days off, and began to focus on the next event looming on the horizon.

Due to many more opportunities to talk about creativity, today I do not have time for contemplative, obsessive preparation. What has changed is my *relationship* to the process. I still do the research, outlines, handouts, and slides. I now (or more often than not) surrender, and trust that, though I am responsible, I am not ultimately in charge. If I show up prepared with a spirit of service, ready to have a great time with my audience, nothing can go wrong. If I had not changed my relationship to speaking and consulting work through surrendering some control, I would soon be nervous breakdown material.

Surrendering is not a one-shot deal. We may need to do it 200 times each day. The good news is that we do not need our own private woods or beach-front property to find the serenity necessary to TRUST THE PROCESS; the opportunity is there for us in chaos and calm alike.

And it also helps to be reminded **DON'T THINK ABOUT IT**. Many of us experience life on an intellectual level, even if we do not fancy ourselves "intellectuals." We analyze, theorize, and philosophize until we are paralyzed. While this may give us an illusion of control, it is ultimately debilitating.

When we are in touch with our Essence and follow our passion, the full mystery of the life process unfolds before us. Had I not been doing so much *thinking* during *Rituals*, and done a little more *being,* I might have noticed that the process was trying to tell me something. I simply chose not to listen. It helps me, too, to admit that it was a choice. By claiming responsibility for my experience, I also claim the all important "respond-ability." I do not have to be a victim of circumstances, at the mercy of whatever life offers. Next time, I may even choose to do things differently.

CHAPTER SEVEN

Embrace Chaos

Michael remembers his experience as a child, moving to a new school in a new neighborhood, always being an outsider, never quite fitting in. "I hated school and I was always getting in trouble." There was a turning point, though. While many memories have faded, Michael remembers every detail of his fourth grade geometry class and teacher. "I sat in the front row and, instead of paying attention to the teacher, I was in my own little world. I made paper airplanes during the entire class. Rather than discipline me, my teacher, Mrs. Rubenstien, saw a doorway into my little world, and instead of trying to shut me down and make me behave in the 'right' way, she used my interest in airplanes as a way to get me excited about learning. She used the angles in my planes to teach me about triangles and other concepts in geometry. It was the first time anyone really appreciated my interests. It really opened me up to learning."

THE PRINCIPLE

Life is change. This is not a metaphor. If we are not changing or experiencing change, we are not living. This chapter is about finding the opportunities in change and chaos, just as Michael's teacher did in her fourth grade classroom. We experience chaos every day on one level or another and often expend much wasted energy battling against it.

EMBRACE CHAOS often elicits uncomfortable chuckles when I first present it to business people. Scientists now understand that natural systems have a life of their own. They need to move through periods of chaos, or what looks like chaos, to reach a higher level of order. When that process is interrupted, the system breaks down or mutates into something else entirely.

Chaos is persistent instability.[51] Newtonian physics tells us that if we know all of the variables of a system at one point in time, we can later predict the behavior of that system. When the initial conditions cannot be completely known, it becomes impossible to make accurate predictions about a system. It *is* possible to see patterns of behavior of the system as a whole, which tells us that there are certain self-organizing principles at work. Weather patterns, population growth, and fluctuations in the stock market are a few examples of such chaotic systems.

Though chaos is largely a mathematical science, here I use it as an analogy to illuminate the creative process, and draw on two of the most important (and paradoxical) aspects of chaos: persistent instability (constant, unpredictable change) and self-organization (integrity maintained in the midst of change).

Scientists use a key self-regulatory process called "feedback" to describe the fluctuations in fish populations and other chaotic systems. In an isolated pond with abundant food and without predators, fish populations grow quickly. At a certain point they become so large that there is no longer enough food to go around. This provides the natural feedback to the population growth, which soon begins to decrease in response to the food shortage.[52] The same happens in processes ranging from gas prices to the human heartbeat; the system reaches a point of maximum expansion or effort and then contracts. This is what is meant by a self-organizing system. Some systems reach a new equilibrium altogether, without returning to the previous state. There is no need to control this process, because it naturally regulates itself.

Rather than look at these fluctuations as signs of system breakdown, scientists now see them as part of systemic evolution, necessary to the well-being of a system. Ary Goldberger at Harvard Medical School found that the heart rhythms of healthy patients are, in fact, more chaotic than those of heart attack patients. He concluded that "chaos gives the human body the flexibility to respond to different kinds of stimuli…."[53]

We, too, can develop the flexibility and stamina to respond to chaos in our lives by becoming fluent in the language of the creative process. The self-organizing power of natural systems teaches us much about the apparent reckless and unpredictable nature of life. Looking at the small picture it is difficult to find meaning in our daily challenges, set-backs, or even in our triumphs.

We all experience chaos in our lives—periods when everything seems up for grabs. Perhaps we are laid off, experience ill health, or find a key relationship in transition. In the moment, it is difficult to appreciate the value of such chaos, with all of its emotional, physical, and spiritual turmoil. Yet, when we get to the other side of these difficult periods, we often appreciate their value. We gain new insights or we see that, though we would never have *planned* the events that took place, they led us to exactly where we needed to be. In fact, it was crucial for us to move through the chaos to reach our own higher level of order.

Cynthia Norris was looking forward to hosting a small family reunion at her house, even though she had major work deadlines and a research paper due for a class. Soon the "small" gathering grew from six to eighteen and, by the day of the reunion, to forty.

Fortunately, I had spent some quiet time the week before thinking about how I might be able to apply the principle of EMBRACE CHAOS to the week ahead. I knew that there would be lots of activity and lots of tasks and felt that, as hostess, a good portion of the responsibility for the reunion's success rested on my shoulders. But I also wanted to enjoy the company of our guests, savor my elderly mother-in-law's joy at being surrounded by children, grandchildren, nieces and nephews, and be lifted up by the jam sessions that evolve whenever my husband and his two brothers have the opportunity to get together with their guitars, banjos, and mandolin.

So, EMBRACE CHAOS I did! When we ran out of cooler space for beverages and still had two cases of beer to ice. Rather than panic, I looked around the yard, spotted the wheelbarrow, and suggested that we hose it down and fill it with ice. Brilliant execution! When my brother-in-law and his wife showed up at the fence beaming ear-to-ear with "Yippy" on a leash, instead of fuming over the imposition, we introduced Yippy (whose real name is Rusty, but Yippy is much more appropriate) to our sheltie and set up a "dog corner" in the shade for the two of them to enjoy the dog's life while the human guests partied on. Nice job! When my two young nieces were looking sad and bored the afternoon before the big party, I put aside my task list, spontaneously loaded them into the car, and took them to a petting zoo and the ice cream parlor. It only took an hour or two, and wouldn't you know that someone else pitched in while we were gone and checked off a couple of things from the "to do's."

My ability to apply EMBRACE CHAOS enhanced the quality of my life and of my family's life. We all, myself included, have wonderful memories of children drinking melted ice out of the wheel barrow, of three brothers circled around candles' glow strumming bluegrass tunes, and of four generations of a family sharing memories and relating the rich stories of their recent histories.

Rather than fight the *natural* chaos that evolves whenever people come together, Cynthia embraced it, participated in it, and enjoyed all of the gifts it had to offer.

Margaret Wheatley and Myron Kellner-Rogers in their elegant book, *A Simpler Way*, describe chaos in terms of "messes."

> *Life uses messes to get to well-ordered solutions.*
> *Life doesn't seem to share our desires for efficien-*
> *cy or neatness. It uses redundancy, fuzziness,*
> *dense webs of relationships, and unending trials*
> *and errors to find what works.*[54]

Those "messes" that we want to avoid, control, or deny are exactly the stuff from which life and growth emerge. Chaos stirs up our pot and gives us new information, combinations, and options that we cannot see when all of the "good stuff" is settled at the bottom.

Another former student shared a story of a series of unexpected, and initially unwelcome, events in her life. After several years of enjoying, what she experienced as, a happy marriage, her husband came home from work one night and said "we need to talk." My student reported:

> *I was rather excited because I thought we had*
> *needed to talk for some time but was never able*
> *to get him to participate. We sat in the living*
> *room and in a matter of maybe two minutes, he*
> *said he no longer loved me; he no longer wanted*
> *to be married; and he had seen a lawyer and*
> *filed for divorce. I was speechless. I could not*
> *even react.*

Despite her attempts to find an alternative, the divorce went through. Not long afterward, my student's company closed the local office and asked her to leave the only community she had ever known and relocate to Chicago. Though this brought more loss to accept, this time she welcomed the change.

> *The timing was perfect, nothing was holding me*
> *back. As a result of the events of my divorce and*

recovery, so to speak, I feel I have become a very different person. I have tried to learn from my mistakes, rather than become bitter or overly cautious as a result of them. I have continued my education and developed my career to a greater level than I ever imagined possible. And I no longer set limitations for myself. If I think it's worth pursuing, I pursue.

My student found the opportunities in apparent chaos. It was the "feedback" that took her to a new level of fulfillment. Had she battled the unexpected (and inevitable) changes, she would have missed the opportunities; she would have interrupted the natural flow of her life process.

Artists know about chaos. It is integral to the creation of any new work. In the collaborative development of new shows, I have found that chaos often emerges mid-way into the development process. Everything we thought we knew about our vision of the show becomes fuzzy and we go through a period of seemingly knowing less than when we started. When we continue to participate in the process and make new discoveries, we move through the fog into greater clarity. Soon the piece presents itself to us again, richer and more fully formed than ever before.

Despite the number of times I have experienced chaos during the creative process, I still have a knee-jerk (and, I believe, learned) response of fear and a desire to control. "This will be the one time things won't work out," I tell myself, "Maybe I should sit down and 'figure out' where we went 'wrong' and get this thing back on track." Fortunately, except for the notable exception of *Rituals*, these have been fleeting impulses. I soon remember that I have been here before and, if I TRUST THE PROCESS and allow it to move through these crucial "growing pains," I will discover the full potential of the creation.

Obstacles make stories interesting. We are brought to the edge of our seats as we watch the characters meet and overcome their challenges. The closer they come to failure before escaping what appears to be certain doom, the more engaged we are. It's not the obstacles themselves that intrigue us, but the excitement of watching others over-come them and sharing in the triumph and wisdom that comes with victory. After all, what good is moving through chaos if we do not learn anything from our trials—if it does not take us to new heights?

Chaos is often a catalyst for building community, as well. In response to a crisis, whether a large scale company disaster or an unexpected problem affecting a family, people often come together for mutual support. The stories that touch us are those of extraordinary character drawn out during such crisis. The bonds that form by weathering chaos together are long-lasting—the framework of a true community, one that is able to *commune.*

With all of the opportunities in chaos, one might think we would welcome it. Most of us, however, have lost our fluency and flexibility to respond to such opportunities. Instead of *embracing* chaos, we brace for chaos. Yet again, we may have picked up still more:

LEARNED BLOCKS

The blocks that tell us not to TRUST THE PROCESS also cut us off from taking advantage of the power of chaos. They are fear and illusion of control. In addition, we learned **DISOR-DER IS BAD**. When things get out of control, it is our job to get them back on track—the sooner the better, or we will all suffer. After all, our credibility, reputation, and maybe even our job are on the line. At least, that is what we believe. Unfortunately, these are the false beliefs of mechanistic paradigm which values order, predictability, and efficiency above innovation. It is an either/or proposition.

Nature teaches us to move through these periods. They are not mistakes, but gifts—a sure sign that life is present, that the process is evolving. If, out of fear, we step in to take control, we cut short the evolution—we cut ourselves off from more possibilities. We may also believe **CHAOS WASTES TIME**. I often wonder where this idea first took root. "Wasting time" implies that certain activities and ways of being in the world are inherently more valuable than others. If we clean out the garage or revise the department's budget we are not wasting time. If we stare off into space or browse in the corner bookstore, we are. This principle challenges our most basic assumptions about our purpose on the planet. Yes, embracing chaos may take longer than "taking control"—just as it may take longer to get the entire company's support of a new mission statement or the family's agreement on vacation plans. The result of participating in this truly creative process—mutual respect, harmony, and happiness—is well worth the time and, in the long run, consumes far less energy than if the natural process of the system, organization, collaboration, or family is *not* honored. If we value participation, collaboration, and the life of the creative and/or group process, embracing chaos will never be a waste of time.

We may be surprised at how quickly the creative process evolves when we EMBRACE CHAOS. Sometimes the universe has a much more efficient route in mind than we ever imagined. Unquestionably, nature's process will be more efficient than the time we spend cleaning up the messes that result from a fear-based need to control.

We may justify our actions with another old paradigm belief that **CHAOS IS NOT PRODUCTIVE**. In nature, chaos is not only "productive," it is *essential* to production. With each swing of the pendulum, the system evolves. When these swings are artificially controlled, growth is limited. When we focus on the end result or one rigid vision we miss one of the most valuable products—insight. Jeff Tworek shared the story of an experience that led him to just this revelation:

> *It was the first time that I met my fiancé's parents. Her father is a very up-right, successful businessman who is the president of a medium-sized company. Upon our first meeting we did what was the proper thing to do—go to the country club for a round of golf while my wife and her mom hung out poolside. Going to play golf with my future father-in-law made me a little nervous, but I had confidence in myself, because I was a pretty fair golfer. On about the fifth hole I happened to hook my tee shot into the rough. When we drove to the area where we thought the ball was, we discovered that it had landed fifteen feet in front of a huge tree. After spotting the ball and realizing that I had absolutely no shot at the green, I uttered the words, "oh shit." At that moment, "Big Jim," as I like to call him, looked me straight in the eye and remarked in his Southern accent, "Jeff, that there is not a problem—that's an opportunity." For some reason it was like lightning striking me from above. At that moment I realized, "You know, he's right. Let's make the best of this situation." I proceeded*

to take out my five iron, approach the ball and
intentionally hook it in a fashion that gave me a
shot that landed on the green. Never would I
have imagined that such a "miracle shot" would
get me on the green. If my tee shot would have
landed right in the center of the fairway, I would
almost bet that out of ten tries on my approach
shot, none of them would have equaled my "mir-
acle shot." The lesson learned that day taught me
to accept the unexpected with open arms.

Jeff found the opportunity in chaos and, in doing so, also overcame the learned belief that **CHAOS IS A SIGN OF WEAKNESS.**

This is a block I hear most often from business people. If things are "out of control" it must be the result of someone's incompetence—because *competent* people are "in control." This is a difficult block to overcome, because it involves letting go of the judgment of others, as well as our own learned beliefs. The truly competent possess the wisdom of the process and the courage to let it have the evolutionary life it needs to reach its full potential. Just as too much control stifles the potential of a child, it will shut down the possibility for a creative process to reach its full potential.

The final barricade to practicing EMBRACE CHAOS is **FEAR OF LOSS.** Chaos often brings with it the threat of losing something to which we have become dearly attached. Fear of losing a relationship, a job, or our original vision for an idea can flip us into a control mode that suffocates the creative life process. What we cannot see in the midst of chaos is what lies beyond the possibility of loss—more abundance and growth than we ever thought possible.

There is no substitute for moving through the pain of loss. If we choose not to let go in order to elude pain, we stifle life and miss opportunities. The universe wants us to experience abundance. When we release our death grip on what is, we make room for what will be. We make room for:

DOING THINGS DIFFERENTLY

During a 1990 interview on "Good Morning America," Billy Joel said he tries to **BE ACCIDENT PRONE** when composing. "The only thing truly original is a mistake." Joel was talking about chaos and how to take advantage of it. "Accidents" and "mistakes" are a matter of perception. They can be obstacles or opportunities.

Unexpected, radical change and crisis can catapult us into the here and now. These wake-up calls can lead us back to ourselves, our Essence. One day we are going about our routine—feeding the cat, blow drying our hair, catching the bus to work. The next day all that has changed. The street we walked hundreds of times now seems foreign, the once habitual business of the day is awkward; and what we once found comfortable, now refuses to console.

A dear friend told how her experience of her apartment changed after she and her partner broke up. "What was once the cozy home that I looked forward to coming to at the end of the day, became a place where I had to be with a lot of difficult feelings." This "accident" led her to a new relationship with herself. Looking back on the year after the breakup, she reflected, "It was one of the hardest years of my life, and one of the best."

My friend, along with many others, learned to EMBRACE CHAOS by approaching life with an **OPEN HAND**. Release your grip. For if we need to hold on to something to keep it, it never belonged to us in the first place. Open hand reminds us to let go of control in many areas of our lives including work, family, relationships, and artistic projects. Let the sands of life flow through your fingers—the breeze of possibility blow through your soul.

There is always more where that came from, so **LIGHTEN UP!** Do you know how to make God laugh? Tell him your plans! The joke is on us, isn't it? Sometimes the best response when things are not going as we planned is laughter. If we cannot laugh now, our humor will be restored later. When we step back, we see what a great sense of humor the universe has. It gently reminds us that we are not at its center.

Much anger, resentment, and frustration comes from a mistaken belief that things are *supposed* to go perfectly—that we were *supposed* to have a wonderful childhood, get into the college of our choice (or go to college at all), meet the perfect mate, find the perfect job, have a perfect boss, and generally have a seamless, linear, perfect life. When we let go of this illusion, and of the belief that we are somehow owed an apology for all of our disappointments (from whomever is handing out apologies these days), we can get on with life, and even have a good time along the way! You will be so excited that you can't wait to roll up your sleeves and **GET YOUR HANDS DIRTY**.

Experiencing the joy of gardening requires getting down on our hands and knees and getting our fingers in the soil. EMBRACE CHAOS is an *active* principle. It is about throwing our arms wide open to the bear hug of life, even if it's a hot, sticky hug, or one that momentarily knocks the breath out of us. Creativity and life do not happen from the sidelines. They happen in, and all around us. In order to facilitate the growth of any creative process, including that of our own life, we must participate to the fullest extent possible—get dirt under our fingernails, and sweat on our brow. Chaos feeds on participation—complete, sloppy, enthusiastic, sincere, unapologetic participation. Then will the plants grow, the business plan gel, the novel emerge, the paper airplane-obsessed child thrive....

CHAPTER EIGHT

Show Up & Pay Attention

Nancy, an actress and poet, recently threw a poetry reading for herself. She has been writing poetry for some years, responding to the world around her and to her life in it. She writes poems for friends on significant birthdays, and reflects on life's comings and goings. She kept showing up, and one day she realized she had accumulated a body of work—much of it quite good. She rented a room (for $15 an hour) in a beautiful old mansion on Lake Michigan, owned by the park district. A friend from work volunteered to cater the event, and Nancy invited all of her friends to hear her poetry on a Sunday afternoon. She was brilliant, filling us with her spirit in that sunlit room, with sailboats floating by and children's voices wafting in from the nearby playground.

THE PRINCIPLE

There are two ways to show up: over time, and in the moment. Nancy practices both. Showing up over time requires patience because, as Rilke counseled the young poet, "There is no meaning with time, no year matters, and ten years are nothing."[55]

When we show up over time we focus on the *process* of our life, not the product. We do not search for the short-term solution or quick-fix success. We show up to our lives in the only way we can live them—one day at a time. When we show up over time, before we know it we move toward our vision. As in TRUST THE PROCESS, when we do the process, product does itself.

In 1930 explorer Richard Byrd thanked his enthusiastic young student, Norman Vaughan, by naming a mountain peak after him. Sixty-five years after Vaughan promised himself he would someday climb that mountain, he fulfilled his dream—at the age of 88. After the successful expedition, Vaughan told the press, "I want people to dream big, and I want them to dare to fail." He never abandoned his dream, but waited until the right time to take action. Showing Up is not a quick fix—it requires patience, vision, and presence.

Presence is not simply physical; it demands our complete attention, which leads to the second part of this principle: PAY ATTENTION. When we become overly goal-oriented, we rarely give value to the present moment—simply being. At times we forget altogether that we are human *beings* not human *doings*.

To PAY ATTENTION means to SHOW UP in the moment. Zen calls this "mindfulness," often described as "chopping wood and carrying water." When we carry water, we are fully present to just that–carrying water. When we chop wood, we are fully present to chopping wood.

Writer Anne Lamott knows about attention and reminds us to keep a sense of humor about it:

> There is ecstasy in paying attention. You can get into a kind of Wordsworthian openness to the world, where you see in everything the essence of holiness, a sign that God is implicit in all of creation. Or maybe you are not predisposed to see the world sacramentally, to see everything as an outward sign of inward, invisible grace. This does not mean that you are worthless Philistine scum. Anyone who wants to can be surprised by the beauty or pain of the natural world, of the human mind and heart, and can try to capture just that–the details, the nuance, what is. If you look around, you will start to see.[56]

Some years ago I began to hear my Essence: "Look around! PAY ATTENTION." Pay attention to coincidence, to opportunities, to feelings and experiences; and to the response of close friends. I heard increasing urgency in this message to PAY ATTENTION, and I was amazed at where it led me and at the wisdom that awaited.

At times the information was rather mundane. At others it helped me through major blocks, such as the time I was struggling to find the opening for a new seminar I was developing. I took a break from my work and went to the gym. When I arrived, I stretched a bit, then walked up to the stair-climber, ready to start my workout. The digital message that scrolled across the electronic panel read, "Just step right up and start climbing!" "That's it!," I said to myself. "That is exactly what I need to do with my presentation!" Instead of pondering and trying to come up with the perfect opening, I needed to "step right up and start writing!" The world has so much to offer us when we practice this principle—when we simply *notice* the information that is available to us.

There is much power in showing up, in presence. We can experience this in group or community settings where the power of the collective presence allows us to tap into much more than we have access to alone. Whether cocreating a work of art or working individually in the presence of others, the power of focused group attention is great. Beginning creative writing students are often amazed at the reservoir of experiences available to them when they freewrite in a group. One recent freewriting convert reported, "I didn't think I had anything to say, but when I started moving my pen across the page the words just kept coming!"

We also feel the power of group presence in peer support groups. Feelings and insights inaccessible when alone often emerge with the safety and attention of the group. Likewise, many meditators report more powerful experiences meditating with a group than on their own. When an entire group shows up, the power of attention multiplies exponentially.

Quantum physicists have discovered phenomena that, by analogy, reinforce our understanding of community power and the interconnectedness of the universe. For example, the polarization or spin of a subatomic particle fluctuates randomly between two possible directions. Some atomic processes produce two particles whose spins are oppositely directed. Quantum theory predicts that when one such particle reverses its spin, so does the other at exactly the same time. Experiments on protons and polarized light confirm that the two particles always have opposite spin or polarization, even if they become widely separated. Somehow the particles remain associated although they are not together spatially. Whatever reverses the spin of one particle at one location simultaneously reverses the spin of the other particle at the other location.[57]

Quantum physics teaches us that it does not matter whether the two particles in question are across the atom or across the universe from one another. The spin of one will always be opposite to the spin of the other. Neither does it appear to matter when these particles once were joined. Particles that were produced during the Big Bang may now be in the atoms of separate objects, people, or even planets but they still maintain opposite spins. Thus is born the concept of nonlocal causality. Its ultimate extension is that everything and everyone in the universe is interconnected! Unlike cause and effect in our experience, this causal influence appears to act instantaneously. This defies Einstein's theory of relativity, which predicts that no signal can travel instantaneously (or specifically, faster than the speed of light).[58]

Just as the same cause affects the spin of a particle here and on the other side of the country, we cannot always track the cause of the idea or inspiration that comes to us in the shower or while we daydream at the beach. However, when we PAY ATTENTION, these thoughts and images become the fuel for our creativity.

If we draw an analogy from the quantum model, it may also be true that our inspirations do not come out of nowhere. In the early 1980s, Rupert Sheldrake began to explore nonlocal causality using his hypothesis of "formative causation." He discovered such mysteries as rats who, taught a new trick in one place, apparently made it easier for rats elsewhere to learn the same trick. Similarly, solutions that crystallized for the first time in one location appeared to make it easier for subsequent crystallization in another location, regardless of the distance between the initial crystallizing solution and later ones. In addition to these and other verifiable examples, history records many cases of discoveries made in different parts of the world at the same time. How far can this be from the experience of individuals and groups who regularly come to the same "Aha!" at once?

Creative impulses and inspiration appear to travel across great emotional, spiritual, and spatial distances without impediment. The information and creative energy we need to determine our own creative spin is available at any given moment, if we simply make ourselves available to it as we SHOW UP & PAY ATTENTION.

Just as subatomic particles are interconnected, so, too, are we as members of our communities—global, local, familial, educational, commercial, and creative, to name only a few. In any living system the individual and collaborative creative process demands participation, awareness, attention, and *availability*. Organic living systems are open systems which must constantly exchange matter and energy with other systems to grow. The same is true with the living creative process. We must show up to it and participate in it for it to evolve and surprise us. If we do not PAY ATTENTION, the sometimes subtle, sometimes glaringly obvious messages of the universe will evade us. This will not be easy if we are living under the influence of:

LEARNED BLOCKS

SHOW UP & PAY ATTENTION seems the simplest of all the principles, yet it is perhaps the most difficult to honor, especially when we've learned *ISOLATION.*

Withdrawing from friends, family, and from our creative community is a sure-fire way to avoid intimacy—not only with others, but with ourselves and the abundance of our creative spirit. Sometimes we consciously withdraw in response to a challenge. At other times, we simply may not take advantage of the wealth of stimulation and support available.

Our dear ones are most likely to reflect our true selves back to us. Sometimes we would just as soon not see that reflection. Unfortunately, such avoidance cuts us off from valuable information we need to move through our challenges, not to mention from the love and support that only those who know us well can offer.

In high school I became a master isolator while appearing to be a normal, active teenager. My parents were going through a bitter and prolonged separation, followed by a bitter and prolonged divorce. I saw the world that I had always known and taken for granted crumble around me. Though I had wonderful friends, I felt I could not risk letting them in on my misery. I chose to shut the door on my feelings, rather than risk losing control.

It took me years to dismantle the fortress I built to protect myself from those feelings. I began with baby steps, risking telling my story to a close friend or lover and eventually sharing more of myself to a growing community of others who were also re-membering their lives. Participating in community means risk and responsibility.

Without community, I survive. As a member of a community, I *live.*

Some of us withdraw abruptly, leaving our friends to ask, "Hey, has anyone heard from so-and-so lately?" Others isolate by omission. We don't build a circle of friends in the first place; our acquaintances are largely work-related, and we don't socialize outside of the office or participate in other activities where we might develop intimate friendships. Or perhaps a recent move has left us without our familiar support network.

Regardless of the process, the outcome is the same: we stew in our own self-referential juices. Perhaps this gives us the illusion that we "have it all under control." Besides, we don't want to burden anyone else with our troubles. This approach may work for awhile. Soon, however, after our only input comes from our often distorted perceptions, we spiral into a negative view of ourselves and life at large. Our worldview becomes a self-fulfilling prophecy. In recovery circles it is often said, "My mind is like a bad neighborhood. I shouldn't go there alone." Just as quantum physicists discovered that when they try to isolate subatomic "parts" they no longer behave as they naturally would as part of the subatomic "whole," our thoughts and behavior can become distorted when we isolate ourselves and stop participating in our community.

I have focused this discussion largely around isolation as a response to difficulty. The greatest value of community, though, can often be found as we share the mundane details of our lives. We learn more about ourselves. We remember that we are, after all, human—that others have had similar feelings and experiences. We cannot learn these lessons in isolation.

Community is participatory; it demands that we SHOW UP & PAY ATTENTION. Just as the creative process thrives on participation, so, too, does the life of any community. What a wonderful place for us to practice intimacy with and response-ability to ourselves and to other creative spirits.

Some of us also learned **TRUCKDRIVING.** A sure indicator of whether or not I am in my body—in the here and now—is by counting the number of bruises and scrapes on my extremities. When I do not SHOW UP & PAY ATTENTION, I bump into tables, chairs, doorways—you name it—if it's in my path, I'll run into it, break it, spill it, step on it, or lose it! When I'm not showing up, I drive my body like it's a big rusty, dented up, dump truck. I am careless. I'm not worried about scratching the finish—what's one more dent? No one will notice. I back into the garbage cans and shrubbery of my life without concern for consequences. Of course, the consequences *are* severe. I am getting *through* life, rather than showing up for it. I miss the scenery when I am truck driving.

With similar results, some of us learned **MOOD-ALTER-ING SUBSTANCES CAN ENHANCE CREATIVITY.** A creative life is an intimate life. It requires us to be available to ourselves on a level that many of us would just as soon avoid. I believe that the romance surrounding the tortured, starving, and drug-addicted artist has evolved in response to fear of this intimacy. There are too many tales of artists who met their demise through addiction to support the idea that drug-induced states facilitate creativity. Here are reflections of recovering addicts on the impact of addiction on their creative lives:

*Part of the progression of the disease was that I
didn't do what I loved. [My addiction] cut me off
from people and my self-esteem—from my own
gifts. Before recovery, I had some creative opportunities at work, but I didn't know what I liked,
so I ignored it. I was dying. It was a
creative/spiritual death.*

—MARA, LAWYER AND ARTIST

*I was constantly focused outside of myself. I felt I
was responsible for making everyone else happy.
It started when I was a child with my mom and
that just continued. I was always focused on
"How do I look?" and that translated into "How
do I feel?" They had to tell me how I felt. I tried
harder and harder to manipulate the outcome. It
was exhausting.*

—CINDY BRUNSON, COMMUNICATION ADVISOR

*I always thought that being a starving artist was
part of the dues you had to pay. I don't think
that anymore. It wasn't helpful to my creativity.
What's different today is not so much that the
ideas are more fluid or that there are more of
them. What's different is I'm able to get them
done, to trust my instincts—not water down or
second guess my ideas.*

—MICHAEL KILLEEN, FURNITURE DESIGNER

Addicts do not have a corner on the blocked creativity
market. If we have ever cut ourselves off from our intuition
or acted in someone else's best interest, rather than our
own, we have a share in this market.

Each of the people I interviewed described the road
back to their inner joy and creativity as a spiritual recovery

process—a process of peeling away the layers that kept them from fully participating in their lives. Day by day, step by step, they were each able to SHOW UP & PAY ATTENTION to the riches of the moment.

As harmless as it seemed, we also danced with **AVOID-ANCE/PROCRASTINATION**. My friend, Toba, is fond of the familiar saying, "When the going gets tough, the tough go shopping." She's on to something. There are many ways we can avoid showing up and paying attention besides the use of numbing substances. We use other processes to distract ourselves from what Schaef calls, "knowing what we know and feeling what we feel." Busy-ness, debting and spending, sex, food, exercise, work, and other people can all be effective tools of avoidance. Whatever our drug of choice, the outcome is the same—we are cut off from our Essence, the subtle (and not-so-subtle) voices which lead us from within and without. Cindy expands on her own experience of this:

> *I was addicted to my relationship. Everything*
> *depended on how that was going. Growing up in*
> *the 50s you were trained for that. You had to get*
> *picked. You could consider jobs as a nurse,*
> *teacher, or librarian, but you didn't think about*
> *a career. You were trained that you were going to*
> *be a wife and mother. It started out with school*
> *dances. You weren't okay if you didn't get picked.*
> *You had to strive for your external person. What*
> *was going on inside didn't matter.*

Avoidance takes us away from our Essence, away from our dreams. Procrastination is an equally painful form of avoidance for many. It is avoidance with an extra helping of self-loathing and guilt. "I really *should* start that paper that's due next week;" "I don't know why I can't make myself get into my art studio lately;" "I *must* organize the piles on my desk." We procrastinate about things we love to do just as much as about those we don't. This obsessive energy is the flip-side of work addiction; it paralyzes us. The impact, however, is the same as it is on the compulsive worker—it cuts us off from a deeper experience of our joy. We begin to define ourselves by what we are (or are *not*) doing and judge ourselves accordingly.

Again, relief begins by simply:

DOING THINGS DIFFERENTLY

Sometimes doing things differently is not about *doing* anything. So **BE PATIENT**. Showing up is a process. In 12-step circles this process is sometimes described as "I came. I came to. I came to believe [in a power greater than myself]." First we need to simply show up physically. Slowly, we move out of the fog of addiction/learned blocks and get in touch with a deeper power, one that guides where our vision once failed.

Life, and all of its creative processes, unfolds according to its own schedule. When we think nothing is happening, often it is only that there is nothing *we* can see or that the process is moving so slowly, it appears not to be moving at all. If we do not get immediate gratification, we sometimes give up before the movement is apparent. We don't stick with our new healthy eating plan; we stop our exercise program; we don't finish the dissertation—it's taking too long, where's the progress, it's too hard, what's the point anyway?

We forget that the creative process happens one moment at a time. One of the joys of writing for me is that, though I often have less than an hour each day to write, at the end of the week I have written several pages—pages I would not have written at all had I not had the patience to SHOW UP on a daily basis!

One way to SHOW UP in the moment is to **NOTICE**. We can teach ourselves to PAY ATTENTION. The first night of class I ask my beginning improvisation students to take a few minutes to concentrate on each of their senses. One by one we work through them—first listening for all of the sounds—the plane passing overhead, footsteps in the hallway, one classmate's breathing, another's rustling clothes, a pencil rolling off a desk. Then we move to our sense of touch—the temperature in the room, the clothes on our body, our jewelry, our teeth, our hair.

When we concentrate each individual sense, we clear out the cobwebs and reinvigorate them. We may be amazed at how many details we were missing. We have all of the resources we need to gather information—we just have to remember to use them! For some, this will be a **MEDITATION**.

Daily meditation is a powerful way to practice SHOW UP & PAY ATTENTION. Set aside time each day simply to *be*. Soon you will find the peacefulness of meditation seeping into other areas of your life.

There are many forms of meditation—formal and informal. Whether you embark on a life-long practice of Zen meditation or simply take quiet time each day, the most important thing is that you do it. Take time to LISTEN TO YOUR ESSENCE, for without this deep connection you overlook the most important impulses of your creative process.

Many forms of meditation begin and end with a heightened awareness of the breath. Breathing leads us back to our center—to our true feelings and beyond, to a place that transcends all thought and feeling. With practice, we quickly reconnect to our Essence by gently returning our attention to our breath.

William Hanrahan reminds us:

> *When we start focusing on our breathing we interrupt the mental process and the emotional process—we change the physical process. That's why breathing has always been taught as the first step to meditation, because it calms the mind, the body and the emotions.... It allows us not only to observe ourselves more accurately, but to observe our surroundings. It deepens our listening, both internally and externally."[59]*

When we PAY ATTENTION to something we do unconsciously, we raise our level of self-awareness. We have choices again; we are restored to freedom and an awareness of all possibilities.

If meditation restores us to sanity, fellowship can restore us to *hu*manity. So, **FORM YOUR OWN CREATIVE COMMUNITY.** Be purposeful or casual. Form a "Freewriting Group," as Paul did. He meets with like-minded friends in his home or at a local coffee shop and brings along a stack of books. One of the group members will open a book and randomly point to a sentence. For the next five to thirty minutes everyone writes a story (or whatever comes to mind) using that sentence as their opening line. Join or form a spirituality group, or a book club, or find a church, synagogue, temple, or ashram that feels right for you, or attend a 12-step meeting (there's one for every interest/compulsion under the sun—try an A.R.T.S. meeting: Artists Recovering Through the Steps). One Fall a group of my friends and I started an informal "Visions Group." We met regularly at a neighborhood coffee shop to share our lives-in-progress, discuss our dreams and commit to action steps for their attainment. The early drafts of this book were nurtured there. We all need a cheerleader or two. Form your own personal cheer-leading squad!

Or ask a new (or old) friend out for coffee, for a walk, or bike ride. Put up a sign at work to find a tennis, golf, or fishing partner. Join a bowling league or go play bingo. Get a group of friends together to make an AIDS quilt panel to memorialize and celebrate the life of someone who has died from the disease. Volunteer to clean up your neighborhood (or someone else's), tutor in an after school program, or work on a political campaign. Or just take a little more time to get to know your neighbors—stop for a chat when you shovel snow or walk the dog. Or take time to visit with a neighbor who is having a slow period during his sidewalk sale or who is planting a garden.

Community is built over time and by showing up. It doesn't matter what your community looks like; what's important is that it's there. You may not think you need a community today, but one day you will. Once again, no one can do it alone. And even if we *could* do it alone, why would we want to? In community we may also find the courage to

EMBRACE MYSTERY.

A colleague at DePaul University recently had an opportunity to do just this. In the midst of a hectic quarter of teaching, research, and committee obligations Marisa took a three-day retreat at a convent on the campus of St. Mary's in South Bend, Indiana. The campus was all but deserted; the academic year had just ended and the retreat house had few guests. The only contact she had was with an occasional elderly nun who lived and worked at the retreat house.

Marisa got just the break she needed—lots of solitude, time for long walks and reflection. She found two big trees on the edge of a field next to a small stream. Always prepared for such opportunities, Marisa strung the hammock she kept in her car between the spreading trunk of a huge old oak tree and spent one morning writing in her journal and enjoying the quiet. As lunch time approached, she tucked her journal in her backpack and wound her hammock around it. She knew it would be safe. After all, she hadn't seen a single soul all day and she was in a fairly remote area.

Marisa walked back to the retreat house and ate in silence with the sisters. After lunch she returned to her secluded spot to find that her hammock had not been disturbed. She settled in, pulled out her journal, and re-read her thoughts from the morning. At the end of her last passage, her jaw dropped. Written with her own pen were the words, "You are headed in the correct direction. Continue on." Signed, "God."

Her mind began to fly through the possibilities. "Who went through my things? What a violation! How dare they!?! Did one of the elderly nuns tromp all the way out here just to give me this message? Who do they think they are? Or could it be that God actually took the time to communicate directly with me?" It was a waste of time to try to solve the mystery, she realized. What a distraction. She smiled to herself and to whom or whatever visited her, closed her journal, and chose to embrace the mystery and wonder of the event *and* to PAY ATTENTION to the message.

Our messages may not always be delivered directly or be signed "God." *And* when we PAY ATTENTION, we see messages everywhere. All we need to do is SHOW UP.

CHAPTER NINE

Make Continuous Discoveries

I have dinner with a friend at a Japanese restaurant. After we wash our hands with the traditional steaming white wash cloths, I notice the woman and her two young children at the table next to us. One of the little girls plays with her wash cloth, first rolling it, then folding it, then draping it over her arm, as if she is a wine server in an expensive restaurant. It then became an ice rink for imaginary skaters and, later, a veil to hide behind. Throughout the rest of my meal, I glance over at the table and smile, as the little girl explores every dimension and possibility of the wash cloth for over an hour.

THE PRINCIPLE

We don't need to be taught how to be creative! Possibilities unfold before us from the first moment we begin to engage with our environment. The little girl was not *trying* to be creative, and she certainly was not *trying* to play. She was, of course, not trying to do anything—she was exploring, making discoveries, and enjoying herself.

Ever wonder why the memory of the first date stays with us in all of its detail for years, as does the first visit to a new city, restaurant, or first day at a new school or job? We *expect* the unknown in new experiences; we have our radar finely tuned for as many revelations as possible. Once the new is familiar, we stop vigilantly checking the radar screen. We no longer expect to be surprised. And guess what? We aren't!

Continuous discovery is wonder. In 1995 the story of the "milk miracle" spread throughout India. A woman went to her temple with a customary offering of milk for one of the Hindu statues. She held the milk up to the statue's mouth and witnessed it drinking. Within hours the news spread throughout the country. Office buildings closed and thousands flocked to their temples. Many of them witnessed the same phenomenon. The next day Indian newspapers trumpeted headlines of the "milk miracle."

It is not important whether or not the statues actually drank the milk (as with all mysterious phenomena, experts immediately came forth with their attempts to explain away the occurrence); it *is* important that an entire country enjoyed and celebrated the possibility of a miracle. This is a creative relationship to life. When we take this attitude—live out of *this* paradigm—we welcome the unknown, mystery, possibilities, the "what if's" of life.

A former student remembered a powerful experience of wonder she had growing up. She, her brother, and cousins decided that every Sunday afternoon between 1 and 5 o'clock would be "the magic hours." During that time anything was possible. She recounts:

It was during this time that we realized odd things would occur; a certain atmosphere would settle upon us and things out of the ordinary would happen. Now that I look back, it was just that we became aware of our creative process and responded to it. But it really did seem like magic.

The awareness of the *possibility* of magic and an attitude of wonder transforms what we may otherwise experience as ordinary into the *extra*ordinary.

The Nobel Prize-winning physician Albert Szent-György defines discovery as "Looking at the same thing as everyone else and seeing something different." Discovery enabled Newton to be inspired to perceive gravity upon seeing an apple fall from a tree. Discovery inspired Einstein to consider time as a variable in the theory of relativity. Discovery led Max Planck to experiment with light, setting the stage for the quantum revolution in physics. None of these people were the first to witness the phenomenon that triggered their inspiration. They *were* the first to witness it with an active attitude of wonder and a willingness to make new discoveries. Had any of them, or countless other pioneers, expected to see what they had already seen or to learn what they already knew, we would not enjoy the fruits of their discoveries today.

The little girl with the wash cloth, the devout Hindus, the children at play, and the quantum physicists all practiced the principle of MAKE CONTINUOUS DISCOVERIES. They teach us that we can choose to create environments of wonder and discovery just as easily as we create environments of predictability, cynicism, and judgment.

MAKE CONTINUOUS DISCOVERIES is the cornerstone of improvisation and stage performance. Novice improvisers often are afraid that they won't be able to think of anything to say or do on the spot. They soon learn that they don't need to make something happen or think of something brilliant. The creative process is powered by discovery. All an improviser needs to do is get out of the way of her creative process and become available to the possibilities that await.

In college I worked as an assistant on Romanian director André Serban's production of *The Three Sisters* at the American Repertory Theatre in Cambridge, Massachusetts. There I learned the power (and threat) of MAKE CONTINUOUS DISCOVERIES firsthand. Throughout rehearsal Serban experimented with new approaches to each scene, to each character, and to the play itself. This challenged the actors, designers, and production staff on a daily basis. Props, scenery, and costume pieces were discarded and new ones requested all the way through to opening night. The actors rarely had an opportunity to run through a scene the same way twice (Serban reasoned that there would be plenty of time for that once the show opened; rehearsal was a time for exploration!). Engaged in continuous discovery, Serban challenged each collaborator to break out of his comfort zone and do the same.

Recalling formative experiences in her career Cherry Jones, who played Irena in that production, described it as:

> ...*one of those productions that is sort of a watershed for everyone.... We were all quite young at*

*the time, and it was just one of those remarkable
experiences that we all look back on with a great
deal of nostalgia. It keeps me from ever really
wanting to do that play again, because I think
we really arrived at that very difficult balance
with Chekhov between comedy and tragedy.*[60]

Actors keep long-running shows alive with the principle
MAKE CONTINUOUS DISCOVERIES by finding something new
in a character, the story, and the relationships on stage to
keep performances fresh. We all perform in some equivalent
to the long-running show—family responsibilities, long-term
relationships, and jobs will stagnate or flourish based on our
willingness to be surprised. What if we each thought of life
as a long-running show that we needed to keep fresh for an
expectant audience?

In the business world MAKE CONTINUOUS DISCOVERIES
has a counterpart in Total Quality Management, which is
driven by the principle of "Continuous Improvement." No
longer is it sufficient to fix what is broken, congratulate ourselves, sit back and relax until "it" breaks again. Today individuals in organizations must continuously look for opportunities to improve each process, product, and service.

MAKE CONTINUOUS DISCOVERIES is a common sense principle
in improving the quality of business, life, and the arts. However,
for some of us it is difficult to practice, because of these:

LEARNED BLOCKS

When was the last time you told yourself, your children, or
a colleague: *DON'T ASK QUESTIONS?*

Many of us had our innate questioning, curiosity, and
mystery-seeking attitude *taught* out of us. Early in our lives

we learned that it was more important to fit in and to give the right answer, than to follow our passion and explore uncharted territories.

Employees tell me that they routinely begin work projects with less than the needed information, because they are afraid to ask "dumb questions." They would rather try to get the information on the sly or figure it out on their own, than appear not to know all the answers. More missed opportunities for discovery! More limited possibilities.

One of the reasons we resist asking questions is a learned block that I find in epidemic proportions: **FEAR OF LOOKING STUPID**.

Where did this deep-seated fear start and why is it so debilitating? In early childhood many got the message that there was a "right" and a "wrong" way to behave to fit in or receive positive attention.

By the time we encounter educational, religious, or other social institutions, we have a pretty good idea of what stupid looks like and an even better idea that we do not want to be caught dead looking that way. When we start our work lives we are experts at surveying the organizational landscape and shaping ourselves to fit yet another set of expectations. By now the stakes may be even higher than before. In many organizational cultures, foolishness means loss of respect, credibility, or even loss of a job. Why would we risk appearing to know less than everything or asking dumb questions in such a climate?

We are paralyzed by **DUALISTIC THINKING**. Schaef says that when we see only two options, we are often stuck in a dualism of either/or thinking.[61] "Should I quit my job or stay and be miserable until I retire?" "Should we take a vacation or invest the money?" "Should I order a banana split with everything on it or skip dessert?" These are all examples of dualistic thinking.

When we get stuck here, it is time to look for the third, fourth, and even fifth option. "Maybe I could drop to half time at my job, while I develop a home-based business or consulting practice or look at flex-time, or job-sharing options." "Maybe we could go on a less expensive vacation and invest the leftover money or have a vacation at home and be tourists in the city." "Maybe I could order the light dessert and enjoy it without feeling guilty or plan a nice long walk or bike ride after the meal to compensate for my indulgence."

These are only a few "third answer" possibilities. Bouncing between two (often equally dismal) choices can lead us to inaction, at best, and clinical depression, at worst. It invites the martyr and victim in us to emerge—and it is almost impossible to see clearly or make positive choices while playing *that* role.

We do not always look for the third option, because we get comfortable (or comfortably *un*comfortable) in *ROUTINE*. Sometimes we stop making new discoveries or showing up, because we are numbed by routine. We walk the dog the same route everyday, process paperwork the same way for every project, and go to the same vacation spot year after year. None of these routines are inherently negative. They block us when we hang on to them for their comfort. We choose not to do things differently, because that means venturing into the unknown—and *that* could lead to feeling out of control or letting go of our familiar way of being in the world.

We all know what happens to our significant relationships when we stop making new discoveries. They stagnate and eventually die from lack of attention. As soon as we decide that we have learned everything there is to learn about someone, that there are no more surprises, an amazing thing happens—we stop learning new things and we are no longer surprised! Ironically we settle into the comfort of expecting things to be the same and then become restless when they continue to be the same.

The same thing can happen in our work. We find our comfort zone and lose a sense of wonder and possibility. Unfortunately, the surprises are happening all around us, but we will not see them if we are not looking. Being caught in this trap means it's time to consider:

DOING THINGS DIFFERENTLY

Counter the influence of learned blocks to MAKE CONTINUOUS DISCOVERIES with the principle *SHOW UP AND PAY ATTENTION*. We cannot make new discoveries without paying attention and we cannot pay attention if we haven't first shown up.

As I discussed in the last chapter, to SHOW UP & PAY ATTENTION we must remember to breathe, be in the present moment, open our eyes, relax, and be willing to be surprised. To create such an environment of discovery is to *CULTIVATE A CULTURE OF CURIOSITY*. This is also a wonderful way to combat the learned fear of looking stupid. Let everyone around you know that questions, and especially dumb questions, are not only okay, but expected.

A manager in one of my classes shared her technique: whenever she hires a new employee, she asks them to come to her with at least five questions each day for the first month. Not only is this a wonderful way to establish communication, it teaches new workers to look for and pursue questions.

Why wait for an enlightened boss to create such a culture? We can give ourselves the same assignment. Look for, and ask, at least five questions a day. Ask questions of the dictionary, your mail-carrier, an on-line resource, the local library, a stranger at a stoplight, the newspaper, your children, or (let's not forget this resource) your Essence.

Another good way to get back in touch with wonder is to go to a magic show or circus. Let yourself wonder, "How'd they do that?"

Discovery also calls us to **PARTICIPATE**. The creative process is an open system, demanding participation to move forward—to be understood. Modern physics made the shocking discovery that, at least at the subatomic level, the scientist participates in the scientific phenomenon. He influences that which he observes simply by observing it. No longer can the illusion of the detached observer or of independent parts exist. Likewise with living a life of possibility. We cannot stand back and observe it unfolding; we must participate in it to experience it. We must make new discoveries during each twist and turn or it will not evolve. Our lives will change, but not take us to new heights unless we make new discoveries.

While you are at it, **CHANGE YOUR P.O.V.** If all you see is what you've *always* seen, maybe you need to change your P.O.V. (point of view). Spend an hour in your boss' shoes (or those of your employee, child, student, customer, teacher, or even your pet—okay, pets don't wear shoes, but you get the idea). What does the world look like from someone else's perspective?

Try doing things differently just for the sake of doing things differently. Take a different route to work or ride your bike in a new neighborhood. Take a day trip to someplace you have never been. (In most big cities you only need to go several blocks to experience a completely different culture). Eat at a new restaurant, or shop at a different grocery store, get lost at a street fair, or just get lost!

The awakening that comes with doing something for the first time jump starts our desire to MAKE CONTINUOUS DISCOVERIES. Perhaps this is what French director Jacques Copeau had in mind when he developed a rehearsal technique to help his actors find new layers to their characters and the story. He asked the actors to put aside scripts and improvise their way through the story, starting with movement only, then adding character, setting, and dialogue.[62] Without lines, the actors were free to concentrate on their characters, the story, and the relationships on stage. They also had no difficulty creating the "illusion of the first time," because it was!

One of my students, inspired by Jacques Copeau, revisited a long-buried passion. As a child she had a natural affinity for sewing and loved to create her own patterns. In high school her enthusiasm was soon squelched by a demanding teacher, who made it clear that there was only one right way to sew—and my student was not doing it that one way. She lost interest in sewing altogether and for years did not return to it—until she heard of Jacques Copeau.

That week she bought a pattern for a hat that would be perfect to wear to an upcoming wedding. She took out the pattern and spent a few minutes studying it. She then tossed it aside, sketched her own, and proceeded to cut and sew as she once loved to do as a young woman. She glowed when she brought her hat to class. It (and she) was stunning. She reawakened her creativity by changing her P.O.V.

She also let herself **CELEBRATE FOOLISHNESS**.
Throughout history fools have filled an important need.
Society has granted court jesters, traveling players, clowns,
stand-up comics, cartoonists, and improvisers license to
comment on, tease, cajole, and "fool" us out of our perceptions and into questioning the status quo. To accomplish
this they often play the fool—the simpleton, the braggart,
the curmudgeon, the baffoon, the miser, the cad, or the
hopeless romantic. These "social workers" have traditional-
ly not come under the same censorious scrutiny as the rest
of us (except in severely repressed cultures). We give them
the same leeway we give children and, as children do, they
help us see the folly of our ways. By making fools of *them-*
selves, they allow us to recognize our own foolishness and
humanity.

Fools help us see things differently—the first step toward
doing things differently. To risk being foolish, we not only
risk seeing things differently, we risk sharing laughter with
others, we risk revealing our cherished human qualities, we
risk deepening our spirituality, we risk learning from our
mistakes, we risk discovering more possibilities, and we risk
having creative breakthroughs. (What was it we were afraid
of, again?).

Foolishness and discovery may not be about playing
with our washcloth at a Japanese restaurant or writing our
own stand-up routine. *And* however and whenever we practice it, it will bring a wealth of creative energy and a
renewed sense of wonder.

CHAPTER TEN

Allow the Boundaries to Free You

Some years ago a woman appeared in a creativity group I was co-leading. Amy was exhausted and starved for what the group had to offer. She had recently given birth to her second child, a boy with Down's Syndrome. Although a trained concert pianist, Amy was having difficulty finding time to brush her teeth, let alone to express her creative spirit. Nonetheless, she managed to carve out one Saturday afternoon each week to participate in the group.

For the first few weeks, the group listened to Amy as she shared her struggles and discoveries. Members became increasingly uncomfortable, however, as they detected a growing resentment towards those who did not have her responsibilities. "You don't understand!" she would say. "I can't take care of myself with kids around every minute of the day." They gently supported her while telling her that they didn't believe her excuses and looked forward to seeing her the following week. The group wasn't buying the "con" that she was helpless.

Several months later Amy arrived radiant. She couldn't wait to share her news. After months of struggling against her responsibilities, Amy had accepted them as boundaries and found ways to work within them. She traded child care with a neighbor and found a non-profit agency that provided respit workers to give parents of disabled children a break. With her new-found freedom, Amy made time to play the piano again and design a Halloween costume for her older son.

THE PRINCIPLE

Today Amy (now the mother of *four* boys) is one of the most creative people I know. She is active in the PTA, volunteers for a community newsletter, speaks regularly at conferences, finds time to play the piano, sew costumes, make cakes in the shape of trains, cowboy boots, and houses—all by accepting the boundaries in her life and playing within them. She reflected:

Making time for myself has required some chang-
ing of priorities in our household (but no one
seems to mind—it was a much bigger deal for
me.) What has been really fulfilling has been my
family's response to me when I do take time for
myself. Because I feel better, they feel better.

Whenever I feel overwhelmed and victimized by my responsibilities and schedule I think of Amy. She inspires me, reminding me that I have choices; if she can do it, I, too, can allow the boundaries to free me.

As with most Quantum Creativity principles, this one is intimately connected to another. Before we can *allow* the boundaries to free us, we must *accept* them; we must SAY, "YES, AND..." to them. "YES" is acceptance. "AND..." is freedom—the play of possibilities within boundaries.

When we acknowledge what is, we can use it to our advantage. This is not unlike the addict's journey through early recovery. For the addict abstinence is a set of boundaries which ultimately frees the individual from the grip of addiction. With substance addiction, this simply means not using the substance. Abstinence from process addictions (in which the process itself is the fix) is not so clear-cut. A compulsive spender cannot simply stop using money, but must define an abstinent "spending plan." This plan is not meant to be a restrictive budget, but a clear set of boundaries within which the addict can enjoy abundance.

The same holds true for all potentially addictive processes—relationships, exercise, sex, eating, work, etc. It is not necessary to stop participating in these processes altogether, but to define a healthy relationship to them. The process of defining abstinence or the set of boundaries that offers liberation is different for each individual.

We often hear dieters and smokers talk of will power and discipline. Freedom from the bonds of addiction or from spiritual stagnation has nothing to do with these convictions. We create much unnecessary suffering for ourselves when we struggle against what is, rather than simply defining the boundaries within which we will find freedom. All twelve-step programs begin with acceptance of what is as the first step: "We admitted we were powerless over _____...." Acceptance creates space for healing to begin, for life to rush in.

This is not to say that the process of setting boundaries and honoring them is a pain-free task. Once we define our boundaries, we frequently need outside help to respect them. I have shared ideas throughout on building community, strengthening spiritual connections, and getting creative buddies, all of which provide support for respecting our boundaries. I do not minimize the struggle of those dealing with the grip of severely progressed addiction. For many withdrawal is excruciating. Even with well-defined abstinence, no one recovers alone.

ALLOW THE BOUNDARIES TO FREE YOU works in the same way the banks of a river *allow* water to flow. They are the barriers that guide, rather than impede progress. In theatrical improvisation boundaries are called "givens"— skeletal information needed to start a scene, such as "who," "what," and "where." In improvisation the givens may come from audience suggestions of a phrase, theme, or topic. Once these parameters are set, the improvisers are free to MAKE CONTINUOUS DISCOVERIES within these limits.

When any one of the players denies the givens (remember George's experience with the boat in Chapter Five?), the scene gets bogged down and confused. Struggling against the givens in improvisation has the same effect as saying "no." It wastes creative energy, stopping the creative process in its tracks. The same thing happens in our conversations and collaborations—discovery stops when the agreed-upon boundaries are denied.

We all have givens in our lives, boundaries that either restrict or channel our creative energy. For some people, time is an effective facilitator—two days to finish the proposal, five months to plan the wedding, three weeks to rehearse the show, etc. Money is often a boundary. Launching a new marketing campaign, rehabbing a kitchen, or getting an education may be bound by limited funds.

Nature appears to be freed by boundaries, as well. Scientists David Ruelle and Floris Tokens made graphs to describe how systems evolve over time. A chaotic system does not settle into a repeating pattern but in the very long term converges to a pattern called a "strange attractor," strange because the pattern is not familiar, attractor because the trajectories of the system get closer and closer to pattern.[63] Chaotic systems allow wide randomness and play, but the system holds together. No two snowflakes look alike, but they are all snowflakes. The boundaries provided by nature allow systems to be locally changing, *and* globally stable.[64]

Intangibles also provide boundaries. Values, philosophy, and vision can serve as guiding or self-organizing forces. I sometimes consult with nonprofit organizations writing their mission statement, trying to define their purpose. They are establishing boundaries. With a strong sense of purpose, an organization can readily enlist support. Without one, members lose focus and morale suffers.

Vision provides a guiding force or framework within which we access infinite possibility. If we take the time to discover our vision, our boundaries, our givens, then the possibilities are—ironically—bound*less*. Each member of a collaborative team may have different ideas of *how* to achieve the vision while the group creative process may yield something altogether different. There need not be a conflict here. Accepted vision allows individuals to transcend their differences. Chaos tends toward order without denying creativity.

Does ALLOW THE BOUNDARIES TO FREE YOU run counter to popular creativity notions encouraging us to "think out of the box," *break* boundaries, and push past limitations? Not at all. In fact, we stay in our "boxes" when we battle against the few non-negotiable limitations. Freedom arrives on the wings of acceptance. We miss the opportunities *within* boundaries, because of this final set of:

LEARNED BLOCKS

Perhaps we were lead to believe that **LIMITS ARE LIMITING**. "If only I had more *money* to hire additional staff, buy a new computer, go back to school…." "If only I had *time* to get in shape, take that water color class, go on a vacation, etc." It is amazing how many excuses we find *not* to live creative, fulfilling lives. "Sure, it's easy for so-and-so" we tell ourselves, "he doesn't have kids, my job, an elderly parent," etc., etc., etc.

When we blame others or our circumstances, we are victims, helpless to choose or change at all. This worldview *is* limiting. When we accept the boundaries, we have choices again. We are no longer victims of circumstance.

Unlimited resources are not the key to creativity. On the contrary, William Rutter, the chairman of Chiron

Technologies, a successful biotechnology corporation, observes that abundant resources can be a disadvantage:

> ...all abundant resources do is allow you to think creatively about how to spend resources...which diverts you from doing the actual research. You develop new programs, build big laboratories, and pretty soon, instead of solving problems in the present, you are just banking on the future.[65]

Ironically, abundant resources can distract us from the range of possibilities before us. If time or money are not a concern, we may not see the simplest, most efficient opportunity staring us in the face. Equally debilitating is the belief that ONLY PEOPLE WITH A LOT OF TIME ON THEIR HANDS CAN BE CREATIVE. This variation on the earlier learned block, "Chaos wastes time," is a favorite for many of us. I hear it repeated again and again in corporations and in my creativity groups. Those who live a life of possibility have discovered that the best way to save time is to stop doing what doesn't work.

Most people can name a few things that do not work in their lives. It may be the after-school car pool, the petty cash approval process at work, or the way board meetings are run at our volunteer organization. While necessary, these are not the kinds of boundaries that facilitate creativity. Yes, the kids need to be picked up, petty cash needs to be regulated, and the board must meet. And, *within* those boundaries, there are many possibilities. By applying the other principles of Quantum Creativity (such as, MAKE CONTINUOUS DISCOVERIES; SAY, "YES, AND...," and EMBRACE CHAOS) individuals and groups can find new ways to do the things that are not working. They can begin:

DOING THINGS DIFFERENTLY

Confusion quickly comes into focus when we **NAME THE BOUNDARIES**. When we are vague about our limitations, we have difficulty finding freedom within them. What are the things that we cannot change in our lives? Most of us have boundaries such as a need to make a living and responsibilities to others. Perhaps we are bound to a certain geographical area, profession, or lifestyle (or are we?).

It is worth scrutinizing those boundaries before we name them as such. Are we unconsciously stalled by obstacles, when in fact there are none? Remember when I struggled with the decision to sell my beloved car? For months all I could see was the boundary of "I need transportation." To me, transportation equaled owning a car. Challenging that assumption freed me to explore other options within my *true* boundaries. Limitations lay only in mistaking the boundary (or challenge) for a barrier.

Once we start looking, it is easy to define these tangible day-to-day boundaries in our lives. However, it can be difficult to define another, perhaps more illusive, boundary—one that can facilitate a deep level of creative freedom. Now we need to **ARTICULATE THE VISION**.

In organizations consensus and universal acceptance of the vision is paramount. It is crucial that there *be* a vision. Vision is usually reflected in the mission statement, but not always. Certainly, as with all things living and creative, the vision need not be etched in stone. It will evolve and change over time. Every member's participation in that development process ensures ownership of and commitment to the vision. Everyone in the organization needs to work within the same boundaries, within the same set of "givens." To use another improvisation metaphor—if I'm standing at a bus stop and you're stuck in an elevator, we might have a difficult time getting our scene off the ground.

Families and individuals can use vision or values in the same way businesses do. Some people are guided by religious or spiritual traditions, others by their morality, or simply by their hopes and dreams. The boundaries provided by individual and familial vision have a self-organizing power. When we accept our vision as a given, all of our energy is naturally directed toward its achievement. We need not strive, control, or otherwise regulate our creative energy in the presence of vision.

We may choose to create additional boundaries to keep our energy focused. For example, an organization that has the lofty vision "to end world hunger," will have a difficult time getting started if it does not set some early boundaries. It may refine the mission: "to end world hunger through community-based agricultural programs." These specifics channel creative energy. As long as the vision leads, additional boundaries will line up to support its realization.

We do not need to have a global vision to improve the quality of life for all humankind in order to benefit from this principle. This principle supports visions of all dimensions, so **WHEN THERE APPEAR TO BE NO BOUNDARIES, CREATE SOME!**

I find it difficult to begin large creative projects (a new show, a course, or this book, for example) without defining some boundaries. This might be as simple as making a "to do" list for the day or as elaborate as detailing a work plan with deadlines for each stage of the process. As I mentioned earlier, boundaries appear in the form of money, time, people, space—whatever amount of structure will facilitate creativity. This varies greatly from person to person. It is important to honor these boundaries or they will have little value in channeling the flow of creative energy.

Lest I sound like a dogmatic, creativity sergeant, again, I emphasize that ALLOW THE BOUNDARIES TO FREE YOU is deeply connected with the other Quantum Creativity principles. Any boundary is a barricade if we do not have a healthy relationship to it (e.g. a budget or diet seems punitive, while a spending or food plan offers hope and freedom). When we SHOW UP & PAY ATTENTION, we may discover that our original vision and boundaries are no longer appropriate. When we MAKE CONTINUOS DISCOVERIES and EMBRACE CHAOS we will be able to name the new boundaries as they are needed. Intuition, passion, acceptance, and trust are all touchstones along the way. Without them, we reduce creativity to yet another set of rules and regulations that characterize the mechanistic system that stifled us in the first place. Within the boundaries, freedom and joy are abundant—scientists make breakthrough discoveries and overwhelmed parents find time to nurture themselves, as well as their children.

CHAPTER ELEVEN

Shifting Paradigms

Embracing a new way of being in the world is not like shifting gears on a sports car or changing hairstyles. Shifting paradigms is a process—and like all processes, as we have seen, it is filled with the unexpected—with chaos, gifts, frustration, wonder and, ultimately, immense growth, power and freedom.

In writing this book I have been challenged time and again to practice what I preach—to LISTEN, to FOLLOW, to ABSTAIN, to SAY YES, to TRUST, to EMBRACE, to SHOW UP, to DISCOVER and to ALLOW. Each principle gave me faith and courage as I faced my piles of notes, and publishers' rejection slips, deadlines, the ominous blank computer screen, feedback from friends, colleagues and editors, and rewrite after rewrite after rewrite.

When I step back from the details of the process, the up-close-and-personal minutiae, I see the process, as well as the *process* of the process—the sometimes imperceptible shifting of the tectonic plates of beliefs and behaviors—the personal paradigm. Perhaps they will be useful when you awaken in the middle of the night, certain that your passion leads to ruin and humiliation or that your misgivings signal that you took a wrong turn somewhere.

When you feel that you have forgotten everything you once knew, take a moment. Release your grip. Breathe. Be gentle. Go to your silence or what you know to be Essential. Rest there for awhile. While you are finding your way back home, take heart in these few simple truths:

PAIN IS NOT A REASON TO GIVE UP

Pain reminds you that you are alive. Sometimes you will lose (almost everything, perhaps). You will fall (hard). You will fail (miserably). You will make mistakes (big stinky ones). You will feel hurt (more than you ever knew you could). You will cause others pain (oh, will you cause pain!). And you will forget past lessons (as if you never learned them). This is all part of the adventure.

And you will get up again, look around, see what you learned, perhaps make a few amends, reset your course, and be on your way again, sometimes making it up as you go along...*and* you will get there. You will get to your full, messy, passionate, loving life.

DEVOTION, DEVOTION, DEVOTION

Do not shortchange yourself from the freedom and power of one-pointed commitment to purpose—persistence of vision. Allow the boundaries of your dreams to set you free to a world of infinite possibilities. Without doubt, your actions will be full of expectant energy, energy that *expects* success and fulfillment. Maharishi Mahesh Yogi was fond of saying, "Just pick something great and do it." Simple.

Your greatness may come to you through devotion to a spiritual practice, a committed partnership, physical fitness, your children, your community, your artistic vision, or a business venture. It does not matter. Value your time and presence enough to give it a clear channel, then stand back! Anything is possible now.

The Spiritual Path is Not the Easy Path

Not easy in that it requires letting go, commitment, patience, and a level of intimacy with ourselves that can be downright unsettling. The rewards, however, are immense. I hope the stories throughout this book give you faith and the knowledge that a creative life is not a magical city reserved only for the privileged royalty we call artists or inventors. Of course, it is not a destination at all and *everyone* is welcome.

Beware of the Dogma

As soon as you think you have found *the* way, you are in trouble. You are no longer a seeker, but a follower. Follow *your* passion, not someone else's path. A friend or mentor's wisdom, religious and spiritual traditions, even the Quantum Creativity principles can inspire us—*enthuse* us—but they cannot replace the universal—dare I say—subatomic, power of your Essence. Most spiritual traditions grew out of the cognitions of women and men who paid attention to the voice of spirit in whatever way it came to them. The traditions that emerged from these great seers and prophets help us find our way.

These teachings, however, hinder us when we forget that we must participate in them to bring them to life. As soon as another's truth becomes our dogma, we give up responsibility for our own path. So, YES!, read your Bible, Torah, Bhagavad-Gita; go to your church, temple, meditation center; listen to your elders, mentors, and wise friends; AND…listen to your silence, your heart, your higher power, your Essence.

ENDURANCE

"In Training for Life" reads the slogan for the Special Olympics. Aren't we all? It may take some time to build up your stamina, but you will get there. Start by walking your creative spirit around the block; little by little increase your pace and distance. What was once a struggle will soon seem a natural part of your life. There is no substitute for mileage, no liposuction to clear away our creative blocks or catapult us into our fully realized vision, just the journey, the training run. It's all practice. And it all counts.

SWAN DIVE INTO YOUR LIFE

Let go to the free-fall of being in love—the grace, the passion, the power of it. In love you are invincible. Your vision is invincible. Trust that success comes with letting go. The diver springs into the air, finds the proper angle and surrenders. You are trained for this dive. You are ready to let go.

LAUGH EARLY, LAUGH OFTEN

We are so silly, we humans. We meet our demise when we think we are important—that it actually matters whether we wear the blue suit or the green suit, whether we order the caesar salad or the baby back ribs, whether we take the job in Tucson or stay in scenic Peoria.

Call your friends in the middle of the night to talk about your latest symptoms of mental illness. *Find* friends who will yank you out of your spin cycle, the hamster wheel in your head. Please laugh. Morbid self-reflection is our undoing. *Yes*, know thyself, but do so in the world along with the rest of us bunglers. Come on in! The water is fine, and we *all* look goofy in these swimming suits.

When the Going Gets tough, the Tough Say, "Thank you!"

In the darkness of personal doubt, confusion, and apparent failure, the quickest way back to the light is gratitude. When things do not go as *I* planned, I rail at the universe, and the universe smiles back at me. If I notice the smile at all, I think it is a sarcastic smirk. "Ha!," it says, "Who did you think you *were,* anyway!?!" But when I open my eyes wide and take a look around, I see that the smile is a loving one casting light on all of the gifts in my life. My restoration begins by taking inventory of the basics (I have a roof over my head, food in the refrigerator; I *have* a refrigerator, loyal, irreverent friends, a love-bucket of a dog, meaningful work...) and then I move to the subtler riches (an afternoon spent walking through the cemetery; my friend's new baby squeezing my finger; the chill from a spring breeze; the sweet, tart taste of a Braeburn apple; a belly laugh with pals as we remember our past fiascos...).

I suppose, at its simplest, my gratitude boils down to acknowledging the at once grace*ful* and grace*less* gift of being human. Sometimes it hits me between the eyes and brings me to my knees. "Oh, I get it! I *get* to be here. I *get* to feel this pain, celebrate this joy, find my way in this darkness. *Thank you,* for trusting me with this gift! " With that remembrance comes humility. Get up again, gather your courage, forge ahead and then:

Give it Away

There is no holding on to the truly valuable gifts, the fruits of living a creative life—love, joy, passion, wisdom, and many others. At the same time, there is no losing these gifts if you give them away every chance you get. Share the universe's blessings with others—they will boomerang back to you, often transformed by the recipient, and smack you on the back of the head. You will wake up again and again.

If you think you have nothing to share—get over yourself! Get out there. Teaching reminds us what we know while demanding that we continue to learn. Be a sage, a prophet. Share a smile, a chuckle. Join in, be human. Tell your story; listen to others'. Be silly and profound. Give it away or you will forget.

Notes

1   Chopra, Audio Tape.
2   Kao, xvii.
3   von Oech, 22.
4   Hazen and Trefil, xii.
5   Leviton, 38.
6   Nachmanovich, 44.
7   Frost and Yarrow, 4.
8   Ibid.
9   Nagler, 257-261.
10   Adler, 15.
11   Frost and Yarrow, 1.
12   Barker, 32.
13   Gribbin, 165.
14   Gamow, 1.
15   McCarthy, 34.
16   Ibid. , 286.
17   Walton, 35.
18   Ibid.
19   *Alcoholics Anonymous*, xvii.
20   Schaef, 18.
21   Anne Wilson Schaef, From a talk in 1987.
22   Nachmanovich, 41.
23   Gribbin, 65-66, 98.
24   Stratford, 93.
25   Milton, 168.
26   Hanrahan, interview.
27   Lamott, 117.
28   *Courage to Change*, 40.
29   Senge, Video.
30   Fox, 19.
31   Peters and Austin, xx.
32   Keeva, 52-53.
33   Ibid.
34   Swimme, 47-48.
35   von Oech, 54.
36   Guest, 19.
37   Ray and Myers, 40.
38   Goldberg, 26.
39   Halpern, Close and Johnson, 47.

40 Lederman, 233.

41 Nachmanovitch, 96.

42 Hayles, Ph. D. , interview.

43 von Oech, 21.

44 Diller, 20.

45 Thiagarajan, seminar, April 26, 1996.

46 Cherry Jones, *Equity News*, 4.

47 Diller, 20.

48 Yogi, 138.

49 *Crisis of Perception: Art meets Science and Spirituality in a Changing Economy*, Video.

50 Rilke, 30.

51 Percival. "Chaos: A Science for the Real World." In *Exploring Chaos*, 12.

52 Vivaldi. "An Experiment with Mathematics." In *Exploring Chaos*, 33.

53 May. "The Chaotic Rhythms of Life." In *Exploring Chaos* , 94-95.

54 Wheatley and Kellner-Rogers, 13.

55 Rilke, 30.

56 Lamott, 100-101.

57 Gribbin, 229.

58 Capra, 313.

59 Hanrahan, interview.

60 Jones. Roundabout Theatre Company Home Page.

61 Schaef, *When Society Becomes an Addict*, 112-13.

62 Frost and Yarrow, 22.

63 Gleik, 150.

64 Wheatley, *Leadership and the New Science*, 132.

65 Perry, 16.

Bibliography

Adler, Tony. "The How of Funny." *American Theatre*. December, 1993.

Alcoholics Anonymous. New York: Alcoholics Anonymous World Services, 1976.

Barker, Joel Arthur. *Paradigms*. New York: HarperCollins, 1992.

Capra, Fritjof. *The Tao of Physics*. Boston: Shambhala, 1991.

Chopra, Deepak. *Ageless Body, Timeless Mind*. New York: Random House, Audio Tape, 1993.

Courage to Change. New York: Al-anon Family Groups, 1992.

Crisis of Perception: Art Meets Science and Spirituality in a Changing Economy. New York: Mystic Fire Video, 1993.

Diller, Barry. "The Discomfort Zone." *Inc. Magazine*. November, 1995.

Exploring Chaos. Ed. Nina Hall. New York: W. W. Norton, 1994.

Fox, Mathew. *Creation Spirituality*. San Francisco, HarperSanFrancisco, 1991.

Frost, Anthony & Yarrow, Ralph. *Improvisation in Drama*. New York: St. Martin's Press, 1989.

Gamow, George. *The Thirty Years That Shook Physics*. New York: Doubleday, 1966.

Gleick, James. *Chaos: Making a New Science*. New York: Viking, 1987.

Goldberg, Natalie. *Writing Down the Bones*. Boston: Shambhala, 1986.

Gribbin, John. *In Search of Schrödinger's Cat: Quantum Physics and Reality*. New York: Bantam Books. 1983.

Guest, Judith. "103 Tips from Bestselling Writers." *Writer's Digest*. Ed. Thomas Clark. July, 1997.

Halpern, Charna, Close, Del & Johnson, Kim "Howard." *Truth in Comedy*. Colorado, CO: Meriwether, 1993.

Hanrahan, William. Telephone interview. 26 April 1996.

Hayles, Robert. Ph. D. , Telephone interview. 22 July 1996.

Hazen, Robert M. and Trefil, James. *Science Matters*. New York: Anchor Books, Doubleday, 1991.

Jones, Cherry. Interview. Roundabout Theatre Company. HomePage [http://www.roundabouttheatre.org/cherry.html]. On-line. Netscape, May 10, 1996.

Jones, Cherry. "Thoughts on Theatre: An Interview with John Glover and Cherry Jones." *Equity News*, September, 1995.

Kao, John. *Jamming: The Art and Discipline of Business Creativity*. New York: HarperCollins, 1996.

Keeva, Steven. "Opening the Mind's Eye." *ABA Journal*. June, 1996.

Lamott, Anne. *Bird by Bird*. New York: Pantheon Books, 1994.

Lederman, Leon. *The God Particle*. New York: Dell Publishing, 1996.

Leviton, Richard. "The Holographic Body" *East/West Journal*. August, 1988.

McCarthy, Kimberly Ann. "Creativity and Quantum Physics: A New Worldview Unifying Current Theories of Creativity and Pointing Toward New Research Methodologies. " Diss. University of Oregon, 1990.

Milton, John. Sonnet XIX. *Complete Poems and Major Prose*. Ed. Merritt Y. Hughes. Indianapolis, IN: Odessy Press, 1957.

Nachmanovich, Stephen. *FreePlay: The Power of Improvisation in Life and the Arts*. Los Angeles: Tarcher, 1990.

Nagler, A. M. *A Source Book in Theatrical History*. New York: Dover, 1952.

Perry, Tekla. "Managed Chaos Allows More Creativity. " *Research-Technology Management*. v38n5.

Peters, Tom & Austin, Nancy. *A Passion for Excellence*. New York: Random House, 1985.

Ray, Michael & Myers, Rochelle. *Creativity in Business*. New York: Doubleday, 1986.

Rilke, Rainer Maria. *Letters to a Young Poet*. Trans. M. D. Herter Norton. New York: W. W. Norton, 1934.

Schaef, Anne Wilson. *When Society Becomes an Addict*. New York: Harper & Row, 1987.

Senge, Peter. *Cornerstones of the Learning Organization*. [Video]. New York and Washington, DC: Public Broadcasting Service, 1993.

Stratford, Sherman. "Leaders Learn to Heed the Voice Within. " *Fortune*. August 22, 1994.

Swimme, Brian. *The Universe is a Green Dragon*. SantaFe, NM: Bear & Co, 1984.

Thiagarajan, Sivasailam. "A Playful Approach to Creativity Training." Seminar presented in Minneapolis, MN: American Creativity Association, April 26, 1996.

von Oech, Roger. *A Whack on the Side of the Head*. New York: Warner Books, 1983.

Waldrop, M. Mitchell. "The Trillion Dollar Vision of Dee Hock," *Fast Company*. Special Collector's Edition, Vol. 1.

Walton, Mary. *The Deming Management Method*. New York: Pedigree, 1986.

Wheatley, Margaret. *Leadership and the New Science*. San Francisco: Berrett-Koehler, 1994.

Wheatley, Maraget and Kellner-Rogers, Myron. *A Simpler Way*. San Francisco: Berrett-Koehler, 1996.

Yogi, Maharishi Mahesh. *On the Bhagavad-Gita: A New Translation*. Baltimore: Penguin, 1969.

ORDER FORM

Fax Orders: (773) 281-1963

Telephone Orders: (773) 281-1901 Have your AMEX,
Visa, or MasterCard ready.

Postal Orders: Meyer Creativity Associates, Inc.
3540 North Southport, Suite 405
Chicago, IL 60657-1436, USA
Tel: (773) 281-1901

Please send me:

_____ information on Quantum Creativity™ Seminars

_____ copies of *Quantum Creativity: Nine
Principles for a Life of Possibility*

@ $19. 95 each* = $_____

Books shipped to Illinois addresses
add $1. 75 per book (8.75% tax) = $_____

Shipping: $4. 00 for the first book
and $2. 00 for each additional = $_____

Total Order: = $_____

_____
NAME   TITLE

_____
COMPANY

_____
ADDRESS

_____
CITY   STATE   ZIP

_____
TELEPHONE

Payment (CHECK ONE) ❏ Check ❏ VISA ❏ MasterCard ❏ AMEX

_____
CARD NUMBER   EXP. DATE

_____
CARDHOLDER SIGNATURE

*Call for information on quantity discounts

ORDER FORM

Fax Orders: (773) 281-1963

Telephone Orders: (773) 281-1901 Have your AMEX,
Visa, or MasterCard ready.

Postal Orders: Meyer Creativity Associates, Inc.
3540 North Southport, Suite 405
Chicago, IL 60657-1436, USA
Tel: (773) 281-1901

Please send me:

_____ information on Quantum Creativity™ Seminars

_____ copies of *Quantum Creativity: Nine
Principles for a Life of Possibility*

@ $19. 95 each* = $_____

Books shipped to Illinois addresses
add $1. 75 per book (8.75% tax) = $_____

Shipping: $4. 00 for the first book
and $2. 00 for each additional = $_____

Total Order: = $_____

NAME   TITLE

COMPANY

ADDRESS

CITY   STATE   ZIP

TELEPHONE

Payment (CHECK ONE) ❑ Check ❑ VISA ❑ MasterCard ❑ AMEX

CARD NUMBER   EXP. DATE

CARDHOLDER SIGNATURE

*Call for information on quantity discounts